Econom

Economics for Students

J. L. Hanson
M.A., M.Ed., Ph.D., B.Sc.(Econ.)

*Formerly Senior Lecturer in Charge of Economics
Huddersfield College of Technology
(now the Huddersfield Polytechnic)*

Eighth Edition

MACDONALD AND EVANS

MACDONALD AND EVANS LTD.
Estover, Plymouth PL6 7PZ

First published 1949
Second Edition 1950
Third Edition 1954
Reprinted 1955, 1956, 1957
Fourth Edition 1958
Reprinted 1959, 1960, 1961, 1962
Fifth Edition 1963
Reprinted 1964, 1965 (with amendments) 1967
Sixth Edition 1968
Reprinted 1969, 1970, (with amendments) 1972
Seventh Edition 1973
Reprinted 1974, 1975 (twice), 1976
Eighth Edition 1978

© MACDONALD AND EVANS LIMITED, 1978

ISBN: 0 7121 0572 7

Filmset in 'Monophoto' Plantin 10 pt. and
printed in Great Britain by
Richard Clay (The Chaucer Press), Ltd.,
Bungay, Suffolk

Preface to the Eighth Edition

The aim of this book is to cover in as concise a manner as possible the syllabuses of examinations in economics up to the standard of the G.C.E. (Advanced) examination and of the intermediate examinations of the various professional bodies. It is hoped that the book will be of particular service to part-time students who are studying for the professional examinations for bankers, secretaries, and accountants. It should also prove useful to students taking economics in the Intermediate and Advanced examinations of the Royal Society of Arts.

The book should be very useful to all part-time students of economics for whom the time available for attending classes, private reading, and studying is necessarily limited. It is not intended, however, that this book should replace wider reading on the subject, but rather that it should lessen the amount of time that has to be spent on note-making. A list of works for further reading is, therefore, given at the end of the book. At the end of each section will be found a representative selection of questions taken from recent examination papers.

Changes in economic affairs continue to take place with increasing rapidity. However, for this eighth edition the book has been thoroughly revised to take account of all important changes that have occurred since the last edition. The statistics, too, have been brought up to date.

My thanks are due to the following bodies for permission to reprint questions taken from past examinations set by them: the University of London, the Institute of Bankers, the Institute of Chartered Secretaries and Administrators, the Association of Certified Accountants, the Institute of Cost and Management

Accountants and the Royal Society of Arts. I would also like to thank the large number of correspondents who have written to express their appreciation of the book especially those offering suggestions for its improvement.

June 1978   J.L.H.

Contents

Preface to the Eighth Edition   v

List of Illustrations   xiii

PART ONE: PRODUCTION AND DISTRIBUTION

1. *Scope and method of economics*   3
   1. The social sciences. 2. The scope of eco-
   nomics. 3. Branches of economics. 4. Methods of
   economic study. 5. Economics a science.

2. *The fundamental principles of economics:*   6
   scarcity and choice
   1. Scarcity. 2. Choice. 3. "Opportunity-cost". 4.
   Types of choice. 5. Choice in different economic
   systems. 6. Scales of preference. Questions.

3. *Production*   10
   1. Wealth. 2. Economic welfare. 3. National
   Income = Volume of Production. 4. Factors determining the national income. 5. Measurement of
   the national income. 6. Economic growth.
   Questions.

4. *Factors of production: (i) Land*   14
   1. Old classification of factors of production. 2.
   Modern classification of factors. 3. Specific factors.
   4. Non-specific factors. 5. Land. 6. The law of
   diminishing returns. Questions.

5. *Factors of production: (ii) Labour*   18
   1. The importance of labour. 2. The supply
   of labour. 3. Mobility of labour. 4. The efficiency
   of labour. 5. Causes of unemployment. 6. Full
   employment. 7. The Malthusian Theory of
   Population. 8. Modern theory—the optimum

population. 9. Modern population problem (*i*) the
world. 10. Modern population problem (*ii*) Great
Britain. 11. Some consequences of a declining or
ageing population. Questions.

6.   *Factors of Production: (iii) Capital*   27
     1. Definition. 2. Division of labour. 3. The import-
     ance of capital. 4. The productivity of capital.
     5. Capital accumulation. 6. Capital accumulation
     in Great Britain. 7. Maintaining capital intact.
     8. Money and capital. Questions.

7.   *The Entrepreneur*   34
     1. The entrepreneur as a factor of production.
     2. Functions of the entrepreneur. 3. The import-
     ance of the entrepreneur. 4. Risk and uncertainty.
     5. Reduction of entrepreneurial risk. 6. The nature
     of the entrepreneur's work. Questions.

8.   *Types of Business Unit*   39
     1. The sole proprietor. 2. The partnership. 3. The
     limited company. 4. Types of company. 5. Shares
     and debentures. 6. The Co-operative Society.
     7. Public enterprise. Questions.

9.   *Problems of the Firm*   43
     1. Co-ordination of the factors of production.
     2. Mobility of factors. 3. Advantages of large-scale
     production. 4. Disadvantages of large-scale pro-
     duction. 5. Limits to large-scale production.
     6. The location of industry. 7. Influences on loca-
     tion of industry. 8. The optimum firm.
     9. Diminishing and increasing returns. 10. Costs of
     production. Questions.

10. *Markets*   54
     1. What is a market? 2. Perfect markets.
     3. Imperfect markets. 4. Highly-organised
     markets. Questions.

11. *Supply and Demand*   57
     1. Demand. 2. Demand schedules. 3. Demand
     curves. 4. Inter-related demands. 5. Elasticity of
     demand. 6. Supply curves. 7. Equilibrium price.
     8. Changes in demand. 9. Causes of changes in
     demand. 10. Changes in supply. 11. Inter-related
     supply. 12. The Interdependence of demand,
     supply and price. Questions.

12. *Early Theories of Value*   70
1. The labour theory. 2. The cost of production theory. 3. Criticisms of early theories. 4. "Scarcity value."

13. *The Marginal Utility Theory*   72
1. Utility. 2. Marginal utility. 3. Diminishing marginal utility. 4. The origin. 5. Equilibrium distribution of resources. 6. The significance of costs. Questions.

14. *Monopoly*   75
1. Perfect competition. 2. Monopoly. 3. Imperfect competition. 4. Monopoly output. 5. Bases of monopoly power. 6. Types of combine. 7. Discriminating monopoly. 8. Advantages of monopoly. 9. Disadvantages of monopoly. 10. The control of monopoly power. Questions.

15. *Distribution: (i) Rent*   86
1. Distribution of the national income. 2. Ricardo's theory of rent. 3. Criticism of Ricardo's theory. 4. The modern theory of rent. 5. Transfer earnings. 6. Quasi-rent. 7. Social implications. Questions.

16. *Distribution: (ii) Wages*   90
1. Real and nominal wages. 2. The subsistence theory of wages. 3. The wages fund theory. 4. The marginal productivity theory of wages. 5. The market theory of wages. 6. The bargaining theory of wages. 7. Wage-rates. 8. Effect of inventions. 9. Earnings of women. Questions.

17. *Distribution: (iii) Interest*   98
1. The payment of interest. 2. The rate of interest. 3. Determination of the rate of interest. 4. Liquidity-preference. 5. The rate of yield. 6. Long- and short-term rates. Questions.

18. *Distribution: (iv) Profit*   102
1. Elements of profit. 2. Pure profit. 3. Causes of dynamic change. 4. Profit and enterprise. 5. Profit and costs of production. 6. Profit and rent. Questions.

Part Two: BANKING, FINANCE AND TRADE

19. *Origin and Functions of Money*   109
    1. Barter. 2. A medium of exchange. 3. Coinage.
    4. Paper money. 5. Bank deposits. 6. Functions of
    money. Questions.

20. *The Value of Money*   114
    1. The value of money and the price level.
    2. Changes in the value of money. 3. The quantity
    theory of money. 4. Some criticisms of the quan-
    tity theory. 5. The money supply. 6. The demand
    for money. 7. Effects of changes on the value of
    money. 8. Types of inflation. 9. Inflation in Great
    Britain. 10. Measurement of changes in the value of
    money. Questions.

21. *Banking*   124
    1. Early development of banking in England.
    2. Joint-stock banking. 3. Types of bank.
    4. Functions of banks: (i) Accepting deposits.
    5. (ii) The issue of notes. 6. (iii) Advances to cus-
    tomers. 7. (iv) Agents for customers. 8. Loans
    make deposits. 9. Bank credit. 10. Restrictions on
    the creation of credit by banks. Questions.

22. *The English Banking System:*
    (i) The Commercial Banks   131
    1. The theory of banking. 2. The balance
    sheet of a bank. 3. A bank's assets. 4. Branch bank-
    ing. Questions.

23. *The English Banking System:*
    (ii) The London Money Market   135
    1. What is a money market? 2. Members of
    the London Money Market. 3. Types of bills: (i)
    The promissory note. 4. (ii) The bill of exchange.
    5. (iii) Treasury bills. 6. The money market in the
    British banking system. 7. The business of the
    money market. 8. Recent developments in the
    London Money Market. Questions.

24. *The English Banking System:*
    (iii) The Bank of England   140
    1. Functions of a central bank. 2. The Bank Charter
    Act 1844. 3. The Currency and Banknotes Act
    1928. 4. The work of the Bank of England. 5. The

weekly bank return. 6. The Government's bank.
7. The note issue. 8. The bankers' bank. 9. The
gold reserve. 10. Lender of last resort.
11. Monetary policy. 12. Instruments of monetary
policy. Questions.

25. *The Capital Market*   149
1. What is the capital market? 2. The financing of
industry. 3. The supply of capital. 4. The provision of medium-term credit. 5. The stock exchange.
6. Method of doing business on the stock exchange. 7. Speculation. Questions.

26. *Fluctuations in Employment*   154
1. Industrial fluctuations. 2. Features of the trade
cycle. 3. Theories of the trade cycle. 4. Full employment. Questions.

27. *International Trade and the Balance of*   159
     Payments
1. International division of labour. 2. Advantages
of international trade. 3. Barriers to international
specialisation. 4. The balance of payments.
5. Invisible items. 6. Methods of correcting an
adverse balance of payments. 7. The British balance of payments. Questions.

28. *Free Trade and Protection*   166
1. Free trade. 2. Arguments in favour of protection.
3. Arguments against protection. 4. Import quotas.
5. Export duties. 6. Regional free trade. 7. GATT.
Questions.

29. *Foreign Exchange: (i) The Gold Standard*   171
1. Features of the gold standard. 2. Specie points.
3. Types of gold standard. 4. The working of the
gold standard. 5. Causes of gold flows.
6. Devaluation. 7. Breakdown of the gold standard.
Questions.

30. *Foreign Exchange: (ii) Off the Gold Standard*   177
1. Flexible (or floating) exchange rates.
2. Depreciation. 3. The purchasing power parity
theory. Criticisms of the theory. 4. Exchange control. 5. Methods of exchange control. 6. Exchange
equalisation accounts. 7. Restriction. Questions.

31. *International Monetary Co-operation* 183
    1. The Bretton Woods Agreement. 2. The International Monetary Fund. 3. The International (or World) Bank. 4. Recent monetary history. Questions.

32. *Industrial Relations* 188
    1. Before 1825. 2. 1825–70. 3. 1871–89. 4. 1900–39. 5. Types of union. 6. "The closed shop." 7. Employers' associations. 8. The trade unions and full employment. 9. Attempts to reform the trade unions. Questions.

33. *Economic Activity of the State* 193
    1. *Laissez-faire* and its decline. 2. Types of state activity. 3. Nationalisation. 4. State planning *v.* private enterprise. 5. Regional economic planning. Questions.

34. *Social Security* 199
    1. Early development of social insurance. 2. The present British scheme of social security. 3. Some economic effects. Questions.

35. *Taxation* 203
    1. Purposes of taxation. 2. The budget as an instrument of economic policy. 3. Principles of taxation. 4. Direct and indirect taxation. 5. Incidence of taxation. 6. Economic effects of taxation. 7. Public debts. 8. Local rates. Questions.

36. *Notes on some Leading Economists* 214
    1. Adam Smith. 2. Thomas R. Malthus. 3. David Ricardo. 4. John Stuart Mill. 5. Walter Bagehot. 6. W. S. Jevons. 7. Alfred Marshall. 8. Lord Keynes.

Further Reading 221

Index 223

List of Illustrations

1.	A typical demand curve	58
2.	Elasticity of demand	61
3.	A supply curve	62
4.	Fixed supply	63
5.	The equilibrium price	64
6.	Effects of an increase in demand	65
7.	Effects of changes in both supply and demand	68
8.	The long-term tendency of prices to rise	114
9.	Medium-term fluctuations in prices	115
10.	Short-term variations in prices	116
11.	A promissory note	136
12.	A bill of exchange	137
13.	Influences on employment and consumption	156
14.	The effect of a tax	209

Examination Questions

The following abbreviations are used to acknowledge the source of examination questions:

R.S.A. Inter./Adv.: Intermediate and Advanced examinations of the Royal Society of Arts.

I.B.: Part 1 examination of the Institute of Bankers.

C.I.S. Inter./Final: Intermediate and Final examinations of the Institute of Chartered Secretaries and Administrators.

A.C.A. Inter./ Final: Intermediate and Final examinations of the Association of Certified Accountants.

I.C.M.A. Inter.: Intermediate examination of the Institute of Cost and Management Accountants.

G.C.E. Ord./Adv.: Examinations of the University of London for the General Certificate of Education at Ordinary and Advanced level.

PART I

Production and Distribution

I. Scope and Method of Economics

1. The social sciences

Economics is one of the social sciences. For a long time philosophy embraced all the social sciences (ethics, politics, economics, etc.). With increasing knowledge the subject became too vast for a single study, and a division into separate sciences became essential. The study of Economics as a separate subject dates only from the eighteenth century—the time of Adam Smith and the Industrial Revolution, when the problems of production and distribution became more complex.

2. The scope of economics

The social sciences deal with different aspects of human behaviour. Economics is concerned only with one aspect of the behaviour of individuals. Different groups of people are employed in the production of a vast range of commodities. They are engaged in production in order to earn the means by which they may satisfy their own wants; and in doing so they assist in the production of goods for the satisfaction of the wants of others.

A simple business transaction reveals the subject-matter of economics. Suppose that a man buys a ready-made overcoat. Its production and sale required the co-operation of a huge number of people—sheep farmers in Australia, cotton growers in the United States, woollen spinners and weavers in West Yorkshire, cotton-thread spinners in Paisley, iron miners in Sweden, iron and steel workers and coal miners in many parts of Great Britain, tailors in Leeds, import and export merchants, wholesalers, retailers, transport workers, bankers and insurance agents. All these people are engaged in some kind of economic activity. A single purchase, therefore, involves a complex economic system.

Economics, therefore, is concerned with problems associated with the production, distribution and exchange of goods and services. A glance at the summary that precedes this section will give the student an indication of the character of these problems. A modern definition of economics is given in II, 1 below.

3. Branches of economics
The main branches of economics are:

(a) *Descriptive economics*. This branch of the subject is devoted to a description of the working of the economic system.

(b) *Economic theory (or pure economics)*. This consists of a body of principles logically built up. Economic theory provides the economist with the tools he requires for his work—a knowledge of the techniques of economic analysis. Theory, however, is developed irrespective of its practical application.

(c) *Applied economics*. For this branch of the subject use is made of economic theory for the study of practical economic problems. Economics is sometimes regarded as a means of solving practical problems. Though an economist is better equipped than others for this task, he can offer advice but not final solutions to these problems, since actual problems have political and social implications as well as an economic aspect.

(d) *Economic policy*. Governments now take a direct interest in economic problems, employing economists to advise them on economic matters and help in the formulation of economic policy. The principal aims of the British Government in the economic field are to stimulate economic growth in order to raise the standard of living of the people, to maintain full employment and to increase economic welfare.

4. Methods of economic study
Economic theory has been mainly built up by the *deductive method*. Starting from a given hypothesis—some accepted fact of everyday experience—deductions are

made. By logical reasoning a body of general principles has been developed.

Sometimes the *inductive* method is employed—that is, a mass of data is obtained from actual experience and then used as a basis for generalisations. This method can be used to check deductions of economic theory. Economists nowadays have the assistance of an increasing collection of statistics covering most branches of their subject.

An economist considers a problem with all the disturbing factors removed. Thus isolated, it is then investigated as if all conditions were fixed and unchanging, as if conditions were static. He then takes these findings and examines the effects of changing conditions on the static theory.

5. Economics a science

Economics is generally regarded as a science, though it is clearly not a science in the same sense as are physics and chemistry. Scientists in these other fields can conduct experiments in laboratories whereas the economist has to study human behaviour in general in the outside world. Economics, however, is scientific in method.

Economists, like other scientists, observe facts, select and classify them, and make them the basis for generalisations. Economic laws are based on the deductions of pure theory, and are valid only in certain assumed conditions. Some of the assumptions of economics are, however, not always realistic, as, for example, the assumption that people in their economic activity are always perfectly rational in their behaviour. In principle, however, what is true of all scientific laws is also true of economic laws. Thus there is no fundamental difference between economics and other sciences.

QUESTIONS

See end of Section II, p. 9.

II. The Fundamental Principles of Economics: Scarcity and Choice

1. Scarcity

The basis upon which the modern theory of economics rests is that all goods and services are scarce relative to the demand for them. By "scarcity" the economist simply means "limited in supply". Our wants are many, but since the land, labour and capital required for making things are limited in supply, it is impossible to satisfy all the wants of everybody.

Economics has, therefore, been defined as the science that studies human behaviour in the disposal of scarce goods. The advantage of this definition is that it is comprehensive and covers the whole field of the subject, whereas earlier definitions did not. Economics thus becomes a study of a certain kind of economising, viz. the economising of resources.

2. Choice

It follows, therefore, that if people have many unsatisfied wants and the means for satisfying only some of them they are faced with the problem of having to make a choice. Every person makes his or her own choice, and must forgo some of the things desired in order to enjoy those considered to be more pressing. Whether he makes a good or bad choice is not the concern of economics but of ethics.

Every man has to decide how to distribute his expenditure among the various goods and services he wants, but the problem of choice also enters into such questions as deciding how to spend his time. Obviously everyone's time is limited to twenty-four hours a day, and it is a frequent complaint by some people that they have not time to do many things which they would like to do. By this they really mean that these are the things they have sacrificed in order to spend the time in some more desirable alternative way.

This choice between alternatives is the fundamental principle underlying all economic activity. Though many decisions may appear to be made from habit or on the spur of the moment, nevertheless even in such cases in effect a choice is made.

3. "Opportunity-cost"

It is clear then that the satisfaction of one want involves the sacrifice of another. If a man has to choose between foreign travel and owning a car the real cost of his holiday abroad, if he chooses that alternative, will be the car that he has to go without. If a student gives up his tennis in order to study for an examination the cost of his study to him will be the pleasure of playing tennis that he had to forgo.

Thus the cost of one thing is really the alternatives that have to be forgone in order to enjoy it. Real cost, in the sense of the forgone alternative, is known as "opportunity-cost".

4. Types of choice

Most economic problems, therefore, resolve themselves into questions of choice:

(a) *Personal decisions* such as:

(i) the distribution of his income between expenditure and saving;

(ii) the distribution of his expenditure among different goods and services;

(iii) the distribution of his leisure time among his various spare-time activities, entertaining, sport, the theatre, reading, etc.

(b) *Business decisions:* A businessman must decide what he intends to produce and what methods of production he proposes to adopt. It may be possible to employ more capital and less labour or less capital and more labour. If so, a choice must be made. Every country, however rich, has only a limited quantity of resources, which can be applied to alternative uses, and thus a choice must be made as to how these resources shall be employed.

5. Choice in different economic systems

Businessmen are constantly having to make choices, such as what to produce and what methods of production to adopt. The way in which these decisions will be made depends on whether the State undertakes production or whether industry is under private enterprise. In either case the problem of making a choice has to be faced.

In a free economy it is the demand of consumers that ultimately decides what shall be produced. A change in demand for a commodity will bring about an expansion or contraction of its output. In this case, therefore, choice lies with consumers.

On the other hand, in a State-planned economy, it is the Government that decides what shall be produced, and so choice lies with the State.

Most countries at the present day have mixed systems, some production being left to private enterprise and some being undertaken by the State. The size of the public and private sectors varies between one country and another. Choice, however, is fundamental whatever type of economic system is favoured.

6. Scales of preference

The making of a choice between alternatives implies that each individual has a scale of preferences—that is, that he arranges his various unsatisfied wants in a certain order, placing those he considers more urgent higher up on his scale than those he considers to be less pressing.

A scale of preferences simply arranges a person's wants in the order of the relative importance which he attaches to them.

Few people, however, could construct a scale of preference for their own particular wants, but in their economic activity they act as if they had such a scale.

QUESTIONS

1. What is meant by saying that economics is a social science?

2. How true are economic laws?

3. "Economics is a study of scarcity and choice." Examine this definition. (C.I.S. Inter.)

4. "Choice between alternatives is fundamental to all economic activity." Compare the means by which this choice is exercised in a "free society" and in a "planned economy". (I.B.)

5. "True cost is sacrificed alternative." Discuss, with examples. (G.C.E. Adv.)

III. Production

Production is one of the main divisions of economics. The aim of all production is to satisfy people's wants. Production is concerned with (a) the manufacture of goods, that is, changing the form of things; (b) the provision of services that have to do with goods, such as transport, wholesaling, and retailing, that is, changing the situation of things in space or time; and (c) the provision of direct or personal services, such as those of doctors, barristers, actors, etc. All these services increase the volume of production. Thus, the aim of production is to increase material well-being, that is, economic welfare.

1. Wealth

By wealth is meant a stock of goods existing at a given time that have money value. Such goods must (a) possess utility, i.e. give satisfaction; (b) be limited in supply; and (c) be marketable, though not necessarily be offered for sale. The stained glass in the windows of York Minster would fit this definition, although it would be impossible to assign a precise money value to them.

Three types of ownership of wealth can be distinguished:

(a) Personal wealth comprising personal belongings such as clothes, jewellery, household goods, etc.

(b) Business wealth—factory buildings, machinery, raw materials, means of transport. These things are usually called capital goods.

(c) Social wealth, that is, wealth owned collectively by the community—schools, public libraries and the assets of the nationalised industries.

The wealth of a country. In calculating the total wealth of a country only real assets, such as those listed above, must be counted. The amount of money, unless it consists of metal coins, adds nothing to the total wealth of a country. Government stocks, such as consols, are simply Government debt, and so cannot be regarded as part of a country's wealth. To the individual, however, money, whatever form it takes, is a claim to wealth.

2. Economic welfare

The economic welfare of a people depends on:

(a) the total volume of production. It is important therefore, to expand output as much as possible;

(b) the distribution of the goods and services so produced among the people.

If the volume of production increases more rapidly than the population there will be a rise in the *average* standard of living. Economic welfare too, will generally be increased the less the inequality of incomes.

3. National income = volume of production

The national income is the money value of all goods and services produced in a certain period. A second method of calculation is to add together all incomes derived from economic activity. Thus, the national income and the volume of production are the same thing, since the amount paid for a commodity comprises the payments made to factors of production for their services in producing it. A third method of calculation is to take the total expenditure of individuals and public authorities and add to it the total saving of individuals and institutions.

4. Factors determining the national income

The volume of production depends on:

(a) The extent and quality of a country's resources in land, labour and capital. At any given time these are limited in amount (i.e. they are scarce), but their quality can be improved.

(b) The state of technical knowledge. Technical progress may be slow or rapid. Progress has been faster since 1945 than in any previous time in history.

(c) The political organisation of the country. Production will be greater in a country with a stable government than in one subject to internal unrest.

(d) In a predominantly agricultural country vagaries of the weather may have an important effect on the volume of production.

5. Measurement of the national income
The reason for measuring the national income is that it is the best measure of a country's economic progress. The task, however, is beset with difficulties:

(a) *Information is incomplete* for many countries.

(b) *Prices change.* Comparison between one year and another is impossible unless allowance is made for changes in prices.

(c) *Double counting.* Care has to be taken to avoid counting any product twice. The cost of the raw materials and the cost of the finished product, for example, must not both be counted.

(d) *Depreciation.* This must be allowed for if the aim is to measure the net national income, and so an allowance has to be made to cover the renewal and replacement of worn-out capital equipment.

(e) *Unpaid services.* No account is taken of services which people perform for themselves or perform free of charge for others, as for example, when a joiner does a piece of work for a friend. No allowance either is made for work done by housewives.

(f) *Foreign payments and receipts.* These must be subtracted from (or added to) the total.

6. Economic growth
Since 1941 the British government has been interested in the size of the national income as an indicator of the rate of economic growth. Table I shows the national income in terms of current prices after allowance has been made for depreciation. For Table II 1970 has been adopted as

the base year, the national income for other years being recalculated in terms of prices ruling in that year.

Thus, if the actual output of goods and services of one year is to be compared with another, Table II must be used. To assess the rise in the standard of living during this period the increase in the population would also have to be taken into account.

TABLE I			TABLE II	
Year	£ million		Year	£ million
1950	10,786		1950	26,305
1960	21,883		1960	34,228
1962	24,872		1962	35,900
1964	29,163		1964	38,080
1966	33,042		1966	39,753
1968	37,333		1968	41,687
1970	43,012		1970	43,012
1972	49,468		1972	44,764
1974	66,512		1974	47,171
1976	96,700		1976	47,800

QUESTIONS

1. How, if at all, is "wealth", as that word is defined by economists, related to the welfare of the citizens comprising the community? (G.C.E. Ord.)

2. What are the main factors determining the real national income of a country? (G.C.E. Adv.)

3. Summarise the main factors determining the national income of Great Britain and indicate some of the difficulties encountered in measuring the national income. (I.B.)

IV. Factors of Production: (i) Land

1. Old classification of factors of production

Any agent that contributes to production can be considered a factor of production. Economists formerly classified factors of production in three rigidly defined groups—land, labour and capital—to which later a fourth factor, that of the entrepreneur (or enterprise), was added. Except where the most primitive methods are employed, all four factors of production are required in the production of a commodity.

The following objections have been raised to the older method of classifying the factors of production:

(a) there are many types of each factor and these are not perfect substitutes for each other;

(b) one factor can often to some extent be substituted for another, e.g. less labour and more capital may be used, or more labour and less capital. It is often easier to do this than to substitute one type of a factor for another type of the same factor.

2. Modern classification of factors

Economically there is little difference between one factor and another. To the organiser (the entrepreneur—*see* p. 34) land, labour, and capital all appear in the same light, merely as masses of resources, quantities of which he requires to carry out his productive purposes. Factors can therefore be classified as specific and non-specific, this form of classification having the advantage over the older method by emphasising the similarity of factors by putting some types of land, labour and capital in each group.

3. Specific factors

These are factors of a specialised kind that can be used

only for particular purposes and cannot easily be adjusted to serve alternative purposes.

(a) Some land is specific, e.g. moorland country is often suitable only for sheep.

(b) Some labour is fairly specific, especially if a long period of training or special skill is required, as in the case of doctors, artists, draughtsmen, barristers.

(c) Some capital is specific. Much modern intricate machinery can be used only for the purpose for which it was devised. Partly manufactured goods can generally be used only for the purpose intended when the earlier processes of manufacture were undertaken.

4. Non-specific factors
These are factors that are not specialised and so can more easily be put to alternative uses.

(a) Most land is capable of alternative employment, grazing, agriculture, building.

(b) Unskilled labour is generally non-specific.

(c) Some capital is non-specific. Some machinery can easily be adjusted to serve another purpose. Raw materials are usually non-specific, and partly finished manufactured goods are less specific the further they are from completion.

5. Land
Land as a factor of production includes all kinds of natural resources, but perhaps its main service is the provision of space where production can be carried on.

Industries primarily dependent on land include all the extractive occupations—farming, mining, quarrying and fishing. Ricardo and his followers considered land as a distinct factor of production because they believed it to differ fundamentally from the other factors of production in the following ways:

(a) Land was said to be strictly fixed in quantity. This, however, is not quite true for (i) land has been reclaimed from the sea as in the Netherlands and some land has been lost by coast erosion; (*ii*) land previously of little or no economic value has been brought into cultivation by irrigation, and this is equivalent to increasing the amount of land;

(*b*) Land was said to be a gift of nature, whereas capital had itself to be produced. Little land, however, yields a return without the assistance of other factors of production, e.g. though Man is not responsible for the location of oil, it is necessary to employ labour and capital to extract it;

(*c*) The yield from land was said to differ from the yield from other forms of production by being subject to the Law of Diminishing Returns. This view is no longer accepted—all forms of production are subject to this law.

6. The law of diminishing returns

As indicated above, this law was formerly thought to be specially applicable to land. Both Malthus (1766–1834) and Ricardo (1772–1823) emphasised this aspect of land. Applying the law to agriculture, they thought that, since land was fixed in quantity, the most fertile land would be cultivated first, but as demand increased the less fertile land would have to be brought into cultivation. As this process continued the average yield per hectare would therefore decline.

The law was also shown to operate in the case of a single piece of land, the return from which could be increased by the application of more capital and labour. After a certain point successive applications of equal amounts of capital and labour to a given area of land would result in a less than proportionate increase of output. This can be shown by Table III.

Mining. The Law of Diminishing Returns can also be applied to mining. The products of the mines are wasting assets, and eventually they become worked out. As mining continues it becomes more difficult to obtain the mineral, and so the yield tends to diminish, e.g. the

TABLE III. *The Law of Diminishing Returns.*

Units of land	Units of labour and capital	Total units of output	Addition to total output
I	3	100	—
I	6	190	90
I	9	270	80
I	12	330	60

(*See* the modern statement of the law in IX, **9**.)

newer British coal-mines are deeper than the older ones and as time goes on the coal face becomes more distant from the shaft and the cost of obtaining coal more costly.

QUESTIONS

1. What do you understand by "specific" and "non-specific" factors of production?

2. Why is land usually distinguished from capital in economic discussion? How far is the distinction valid? (I.B.)

3. Consider the Law of Diminishing Returns as it applies to (*a*) agriculture and (*b*) mining.

4. What advantages has the modern over the older method of classifying the factors of production?

5. Explain the meaning and importance of the Law of Diminishing Returns. (G.C.E. Adv.)

V. Factors of production: (ii) Labour

1. The importance of labour

Modern methods of production require the co-operation of all four factors of production. Labour has always been indispensable to production. A primitive people may find its food growing wild on the trees, but before it can be consumed labour must be employed to gather it. The early economists placed labour in a special category, but economically it is no different in its function from the other factors of production. Labour is regarded as productive whether it is employed in changing raw materials into finished products, or whether it is employed in providing commercial or personal services. In fact, all labour provides services—the weaver the service of weaving, the shopkeeper the service of retailing, the doctor medical service.

2. The supply of labour

The supply of labour that is available to the entrepreneur will depend upon:

(a) The total population of the country.

(b) The proportion of the total population available for employment. This will depend on the school-leaving age, the extent to which women go out to work and the age of retirement.

(c) The length of the working week and the number of holidays per year.

3. Mobility of labour

There are two aspects of mobility:

(a) Occupational mobility, that is, the ease with which labour can be transferred from declining to expanding

industries. The more specific the labour, the less mobile
it is in this sense.

(b) Geographical mobility, that is, the willingness of
labour to move from districts where work is difficult to
obtain to those where there is a greater demand for
labour. Specific labour appears generally to be more
mobile in this sense.

4. The efficiency of labour
The efficiency of a country's labour will depend on:

(a) *The physical well-being of the people.* Adequate
food, clothing and shelter are essential for the maintenance of health and so of a high standard of efficiency.

(b) *Working conditions.* These have been greatly improved as a result of the Factory Acts, etc. Particular attention is now paid to ventilation, overcrowding and
safety.

(c) *Social services.* These aid efficiency in two ways: (i)
assuring the maintenance of a minimum standard of
health during unemployment, and (ii) relieving people of
the worry about possible sickness or unemployment in
the future. A comprehensive Social Insurance Scheme
was introduced in Great Britain in 1946, covering sickness, unemployment, retirement, maternity, and funeral
benefits.

(d) *Education and training.* A high standard of general
education and an efficient system of technical education
are essentials for a modern industrial community.

(e) *The efficiency of the other factors of production,*
especially the entrepreneur.

(f) *The extent to which capitalistic methods of production are adopted.*

(g) *The greater the degree of specialisation,* the greater
will be the output per man.

I. THE PROBLEM OF UNEMPLOYMENT

5. Causes of unemployment
Before it is possible to formulate plans for the reduction

of unemployment it is necessary to distinguish between the different causes of unemployment:

(a) *Mass or cyclical unemployment.* This is the type of unemployment that was associated with the trade cycle. It is characterised by a general deficiency of demand, so that nearly all industries are affected at the same time. Before 1914 the trade cycle was a feature of production, but neither boom nor slump was of long duration. The Great Depression of 1929–35 was world-wide, longer and more severe than any previous slump, and unemployment was correspondingly greater. This is the most serious type of unemployment.

(b) *Structural unemployment.* This is an example of frictional unemployment and is the result of changes in demand. Tastes change and the demand for some goods declines, although the demand for other goods may increase. If labour was perfectly mobile its transfer from the declining to the expanding industry would be easy. This, however, is not the case, and so unemployment results in the declining industry.

(c) *Technical developments.* The invention of new machinery, if it is of a labour-saving type, may displace some labour. In the long run, inventions tend to increase demand, including the demand for labour, but this will probably require the transfer of labour to other industries, and again because labour is not perfectly mobile, unemployment occurs.

(d) *Strikes.* As a result of strikes, voluntary unemployment may occur in the industries which are directly affected by the dispute. Involuntary unemployment, however, may be caused indirectly in other industries which are dependent on the industry in which the strike occurred, e.g. a coal strike will cause unemployment in all industries dependent on coal for power.

(e) *Seasonal unemployment.* This occurs in many outdoor occupations, as for example, in the building trades, when bad weather may cause a suspension of work. There are some occupations too where there is a demand for labour only at certain seasons of the year, as with potato-lifting, hop-picking and many kinds of work at seaside resorts.

(*f*) *Residual unemployment*. There are a certain number of people who are unemployed on account of mental or physical disability. Even in time of war, when the demand for labour greatly exceeds the supply, a few thousand unemployed of this type will usually be found.

6. Full employment

Lord Beveridge published his book on Full Employment in 1944. Though his policy was directed chiefly against mass or cyclical unemployment, he also made suggestions for dealing with unemployment caused by changes in demand or by technical change.

Full employment does not mean that every person is fully employed all the time, for there would still be unemployment due to economic friction resulting from causes (*b*) and (*c*), while unemployment arising from causes (*d*), (*e*) and (*f*) would also still remain.

Full employment would, however, mean the end of trade depressions with widespread unemployment affecting all industries to a greater or less extent at the same time. This requires the State to make itself responsible for ensuring that the demand for labour is sufficient at all times to prevent mass unemployment. Many countries, including Great Britain, have accepted responsibility for the maintenance of full employment.

II. THE POPULATION PROBLEM

7. The Malthusian theory of population

When Malthus formulated his theory of population he was greatly impressed by two things:

(*a*) the population of England was increasing more rapidly than ever before;
(*b*) the application to land of the Law of Diminishing Returns as he understood it.

He thought that each increase in population made it necessary to cultivate less-fertile land, and since in his day population was increasing at an extraordinary rate, he felt that a food shortage would be the eventual outcome. The effects of the improvements in farming methods of the eighteenth century he considered to be merely temporary. In previous centuries famine, disease and war had checked the growth of population.

TABLE IV. *Growth of Population of United Kingdom.*

Date	Million
1801	11.9
1901	38.2
1961	52.7
1971	55.5
1981 (est.)	56.3

8. Modern theory—the optimum population

The course of events of the nineteenth century seemed to prove that Malthus was wrong. Population continued to increase rapidly throughout the nineteenth century (chiefly due to a fall in the death-rate), but by 1900 there was less danger of famine than when he wrote. For this two things were responsible:

(a) New areas of food production were opened up— the Prairies, Pampas, Australia, New Zealand.

(b) Enormous progress was made in the development of means of transport.

Thus the New World was able to feed the Old.

The population of a country may be either too large or too small in proportion to the other factors there. For any given area in certain circumstances there is, therefore, an optimum population, i.e. that quantity of labour which, combined with the other factors, gives the maximum output. Thus the test of over-population is whether it exceeds the optimum, and so it is possible for a thinly populated country to be over-populated if it has a poor supply of other factors, and for a densely populated country to be under-populated if it has not a sufficient quantity of labour to make the most effective use of its other factors.

9. Modern population problems: (i) the world

In the world as a whole the problem is still the possibility of population increasing more rapidly than food production. Therefore, after all, Malthus may have been right. In 1975 the population of the world was 4,050 million, and it was increasing at the rate of 90 million a year. The greatest numerical increase is still in Asia, but recently both North and South America have shown greater rates of increase. It has been calculated that by the year 2000 the world may have a population of 6,500 million. To meet such an increase the world output of food needs to be doubled every 50 years. Since also large numbers of people are at present underfed, an even greater increase in food production is desirable.

The problem has been aggravated by short-sighted farming methods in the past in some parts of the world, as a result of which the fertility of the soil has been much reduced in some countries. In the United States soil erosion produced the great dust bowl.

The Food and Agricultural Organisation of the United Nations studies farming problems in many lands in order to try to increase output; quicker-ripening crops make further development possible in N. Europe and N. Canada; in many areas more intensive farming might be practised, and the further development of chemical fertilisers makes this possible. Probably, too, more food could also be obtained from the sea. Nevertheless, the fact remains that if population continues to increase, all these developments merely postpone the time of crisis.

10. Modern population problem: (ii) Great Britain

In Great Britain the problem is still the possibility of a decline in population, though there is now less certainty of this, some people believing that the population of the country is likely to maintain itself for a long time to come.

From 34.2 in 1880 the birth-rate fell to 15.2 per 1,000 in 1934. In the 1920s it was calculated that the population of this country would begin to decline after 1944. In the 1930s the fall in the birth-rate was arrested. Though the birth-rate was higher in the 1950s and 1960s (reaching 18.7 per 1,000 in 1964 but falling to 13.2 per 1,000 in 1974), it is still not high enough to prevent an eventual decline in the population.

The effect of recent changes, however, has been at least to postpone the date when a decline might set in. During the past hundred years there has been a steady fall in the death-rate (until 1964 since when it has risen slightly), with the result that, even if the population does not fall, there is likely to be an increase in the proportion of older people.

11. Some consequences of a declining or ageing population

In the case of either a declining or an ageing population there will probably be a tendency for there to be increases in three of the more important types of unemployment:

(a) *Mass or cyclical unemployment.* It is easier to bring a trade depression to an end when the population is increasing on account of the expansion of demand brought about by the increase.

(b) *Structural unemployment.* Changes in demand likely to give rise to structural unemployment may occur as a result of the following:

(i) The changed distribution of the population within the various age groups—a greater proportion of older people and a smaller proportion of children. Table V shows how the proportion of elderly people in Great Britain has increased during the past 150 years. So the demand for those commodities desired by older people may increase relatively to the demand for things required for children.

(ii) The economic friction caused by change in demand due to changes in tastes will be more difficult to

TABLE V. *Increase in the Elderly Population of Great Britain.*

	1821 %	1941 %	1971 %	1975 %
Elderly people	8	12	14	15
People of working age	65	67	62	61
Children	27	21	24	24

overcome. The easiest method of altering the labour supply in different industries is through new entrants, and there will be fewer of these.

(*c*) *Technical progress.* This causes unemployment in the short period until industry has adapted itself to the new conditions. Adjustments are easier with an increasing population.

Other effects of a declining population would be on the following:

(*d*) *The national debt.* The burden of the national debt will become greater per head the smaller the population, though this may to some extent be offset by a fall in the value of money.

(*e*) *Social security.* This becomes an increasingly costly charge per head of the working population, due to the greater proportion of the people receiving retirement pensions. In 1975 there were 8.3 million people in the United Kingdom in receipt of retirement pension, an increase of over a million since 1961.

(*f*) *The optimum population.* If before the decline, the population was the optimum, the reduced quantity of labour will be insufficient to work the other factors of production effectively. A decrease in population will only be an advantage if the population was previously in excess of the optimum, as would probably be the case in China or India.

QUESTIONS

1. Discuss the economic consequences of a declining or stationary population.

2. What are the main causes of unemployment? (I.B.)

3. "Labour is not creative of objects but of utilities" (Mill). Explain this statement, indicating what you mean by productive labour. (R.S.A. Inter.)

4. What theories did Malthus produce in regard to population? What truth, if any, do you think they contain? (A.C.A. Inter.)

5. Over the long period, the birth-rate has been falling while the expectation of life has been growing longer. What effect have these trends produced upon the age distribution of the population? How would you expect the changing age distribution to influence industrial development? (I.B.)

6. What do you understand by the Malthusian population law? Has it any contemporary significance? (G.C.E. Adv.)

VI. Factors of Production: (iii) Capital

1. Definition

Income is an addition to existing wealth, whereas capital is a stock of wealth existing at a given time. People differ greatly in their conceptions of capital. Some regard it as synonymous with wealth, but if capital is treated as a factor of production it can then include only wealth that is used productively. Capital can therefore be defined as wealth employed with other factors of production in the creation of further wealth. Thus, though capital is wealth, all wealth is not capital.

Producers' goods and consumers' goods. All goods produced, except armaments, can be divided into these two categories:

(*a*) *Producers' goods* are all those goods that are not wanted for their own sake but merely as aids to the production of other goods, especially consumers' goods. Under this heading we should include factories, industrial plant, tools, machinery, raw materials, partly-finished goods and means of transport.

(*b*) *Consumers' goods* are the ultimate aim of all production. They include all kinds of goods in the form in which they are required by the people who wish to make use of them, and comprise such things as food, clothing, household goods, etc.

The term capital is best restricted to producers' goods. In fact, these are often called capital goods. All goods that have not reached the final stage of production can be regarded as capital goods.

At the present day a large share of production is given up to the manufacture of armaments. These are neither consumers' goods nor producers' goods, though their production reduces the production both of capital and of consumers' goods.

2. Division of labour

This means the specialisation of processes. In early times one man would perform every operation required for the manufacture of a commodity from raw material to finished article; he would, too, make many quite different commodities. First, therefore, came division into separate trades. Clearly, a man who restricted his activities to one craft became more skilful at it than a man engaged in several distinct trades. With the development of the factory system, division of labour came to mean the division of the work of production into a number of separate processes, each of which was undertaken by a different worker.

Though it is possible to conceive of a division of labour where little or no capital is employed, modern specialisation of processes within individual industries dates from the Industrial Revolution (c. 1760–1840), when power-driven machinery first began to be employed. Division of labour into separate processes made possible the use of machinery to speed up production.

Advantages of division of labour. Division of labour results in a great increase of output, a pact which greatly impressed Adam Smith. There are five main reasons why division of labour leads to increased output:

(a) Workmen acquire greater skill when they perform single operations.

(b) There is a saving of time between processes, the partly-finished product being simply passed on to the next man.

(c) It makes the employment of specialists possible.

(d) Workers suffer less fatigue.

(e) It makes possible the use of machinery.

Disadvantages of division of labour.

(a) Repetitive work becomes monotonous and uninteresting to most workers.

(b) The workman becomes a mere tender of a machine and ceases to be a craftsman.

(c) Labour becomes more specific and so more liable to structural unemployment.

3. The importance of capital

Production can be expanded by the employment of capital, for it makes possible a greater specialisation of processes, i.e. a greater division of labour. The greater the extent to which specialisation is adopted, the more "capitalistic" or the more "roundabout" is said to be the method of production. Thus, the word capitalistic simply means making a greater use of capital goods such as machinery. In this sense the word is applicable equally to production in a communist state where capital is collectively owned as to capitalism, under which private ownership of capital is permitted.

The more capitalistic the method of production, however, the longer will be the time interval between taking the decision to produce and the beginning of the outflow of the product, thereby increasing the risk associated with production.

"*Waiting.*" This is an important feature of capital, since the capital itself has to be produced before a capitalistic method of production can be undertaken. The incentive to "wait" is the increased output that can be obtained by the employment of more capital. When Russia decided to develop its industrial resources the first two Five Year Plans were both devoted to the production of capital equipment. The Russian people who wanted consumers' goods had to "wait" until the producers' goods had first been accumulated. The accumulation of capital thus takes time and involves sacrifice of present for future satisfaction.

4. The productivity of capital

No production is possible by capital alone, but this also applies to the other factors of production. Since capital makes possible greater specialisation, thereby achieving a vast increase in output, capital can be said to be productive. The huge increase in average output per worker during the past two hundred years is almost entirely the result of employing more and better capital. Automation produces an even greater increase in the productivity of both capital and labour.

5. Capital accumulation
Capital formation depends on saving, for saving makes possible the accumulation of capital. Since capital is a stock wealth set apart for the production of further wealth, it follows that during a period there can be no capital accumulation unless the quantity of goods consumed is less than the total produced. The accumulation of capital involves the diversion of some productive resources from the manufacture of consumers' goods to the production of capital goods. The productive forces thus set free can then be used to produce capital goods. The actual production of capital is known as *investment*. Saving, therefore, involves forgoing present consumption in order to make investment possible.

6. Capital accumulation in Great Britain
Just as a poor man finds it difficult to save, so a poor country finds it difficult to accumulate real capital. In both cases it is necessary to forgo current consumption. A man who has so small an income that he can afford to buy only the bare necessaries of life has little scope for saving. Similarly, if it takes almost the entire time and energy of a people to produce the minimum output necessary for mere subsistence, factors of production cannot easily be spared for the production of capital goods. Once, however, a little capital has been acquired it becomes increasingly easier to save and accumulate more.

All capital accumulation depends on saving. People, however, are not likely to save unless they are reasonably sure their property will be secure. Also, the habit of saving requires time to develop. Opportunities for investment will encourage saving, but mere hoarding does not lead to capital accumulation.

The Industrial Revolution provided increasing opportunities for saving on a previously unprecedented scale. Joint-stock companies, especially after the introduction of limited liability, provided opportunities for many people. In Great Britain conditions first became favourable to saving during the Victorian period. The modern unit investment trust offers a safe form of investment in public limited companies for people of small means. At the present day, however, most saving comes from institutional investors—insurance companies, etc.—or the undistributed profits of limited companies. Modern governments also undertake a considerable amount of investment in such things as house and school-building, roadmaking, etc.

7. Maintaining capital intact

A certain amount of production must be set aside each year for the replacement of worn-out or obsolete capital. For progress to be maintained capital accumulation must be in excess of the minimum amount necessary for replacement. Economic progress demands that out-of-date forms of capital should give place to newer and more up-to-date types. It is not wasteful, therefore, to scrap machinery, even though it be in perfectly good condition, if it has become obsolete and can be replaced by more efficient capital.

Capital consumption. If a country fails to keep its existing capital intact it is said to be consuming its capital or living on its capital. Depreciation of capital can take the form of the wearing out of machinery or the using up of stocks. Even if no capital is actually destroyed by enemy action, capital consumption is most likely to occur in time of war, as a result of neglecting to carry out repairs and make replacements. Capital consumption can also occur if too great a proportion of a country's resources are employed on the production of consumers' goods, that is, if there is insufficient saving.

A country, like an individual, cannot live on its capital without eventually becoming poorer. During a war a country may live on its capital for a period in order to concentrate on its war effort, but in doing so it is clearly taking a great risk. When the war ends it will be faced by a formidable programme of capital production. Since every country's resources are limited in amount, an expansion in the production of capital goods can take place only at the expense of the production of consumers' goods. Similarly, an armaments programme can be carried out only by reducing capital investment or curtailing the production of consumers' goods.

8. Money and capital

To the economist capital is a stock of goods of a certain kind, but to the business world capital often appears to be synonymous with money. An increase in the quantity of money, however, does not increase the capital of a country, though it would that of an individual. Money is simply a means of exchange, and is capital only in the sense that it gives command over goods.

An accountant thinks of capital in terms of money only because it is customary to calculate the assets of a business in terms of money. Similarly, when individuals curtail their consumption it is money they save. Money that has been saved may be used to purchase shares in manufacturing businesses, which use it to purchase capital goods. The individual both saves and invests money, but the community saves by reducing consumption and the producer invests by producing real capital goods.

QUESTIONS

1. Our modern industrial economy is based on the principle of division of labour. Show how this principle has helped in increasing output and mention also some of its bad effects. (G.C.E. Ord.)

2. What is capital? Apply your argument to the following cases: a manufacturing undertaking; shares in a limited company; a house. (I.B.)

3. State precisely what you mean by capital. What is meant by living on capital? (G.C.E. Adv.)

4. What were the chief causes of capital accumulation in Great Britain during the nineteenth century?

5. In what manner is capital produced, saved and consumed? What conditions influence the accumulation of capital in any community? (R.S.A. Inter.)

6. Distinguish between consumer and producer goods. Why is the distinction important in economics? (G.C.E. Adv.)

VII. The Entrepreneur

1. The entrepreneur as a factor of production

At one time only three factors of production were recognised—land, labour, and capital. Due to the influence of Marshall, the entrepreneur (or organisation) came to be regarded as a fourth factor, though a large number of economists now consider it to be only a special type of labour. The organisation undertaken by the entrepreneur is, however, different in kind from that undertaken by labour. Whereas labour is responsible to some extent for the work it does, the entrepreneur is responsible for organising the work of other people, as well as deciding what quantities of the other factors he will employ.

The entrepreneur, therefore, differs from the other factors in being the active factor in production, the others being the resources at his disposal.

2. Functions of the entrepreneur

Whether or not the entrepreneur is regarded as a separate factor of production his functions to production are of great importance:

(a) *Risk and uncertainty bearing*. This is the primary function of the entrepreneur.

(b) The other *factors of production* can be used effectively only if they are *combined in the best proportion*. To the entrepreneur the other factors are just masses of resources, and to a certain extent he can choose between employing more of one and less of another.

(c) He must decide what *scale of production* to adopt, that is, he decides the size of the firm. Upon him also devolves the establishment of new businesses.

(d) What *assortment of goods* shall be produced depends upon the entrepreneurs. They decide what industries to enter and what to produce.

(*e*) The entrepreneur is responsible for the *marketing* of the product.

(*f*) *Control* of the firm is in his hands.

There are thus two main aspects of the entrepreneur's work (*i*) bearing the uncertainties of production and (*ii*) management.

3. The importance of the entrepreneur

Under a system of private enterprise it is really the consumer who decides what shall be produced, for the entrepreneur attempts to forecast the future demand of consumers. The monopolist, however, attempts to limit the *sovereignty of the consumer*. In a fully-planned economy, production is planned by the State, which decides both what shall be produced and how much shall be produced.

The entrepreneur and risk-bearing. The most fundamental fact is how to meet uncertainty. Production has to be undertaken in anticipation of demand, and the entrepreneur must estimate what he thinks that future demand will be. We live, however, in a changing world, and so there must always be uncertainty about the future condition of demand. It is the particular function of the entrepreneur to bear this uncertainty.

The more capitalistic the method, the longer will be the time interval taken by production and the greater, therefore, the uncertainty, since demand can change in the interval. During the past hundred years production has become ever more capitalistic, and during that time, therefore, the importance of the entrepreneur has enormously increased.

The entrepreneur as organiser. Men differ in their attitude to uncertainty in many ways:

(*a*) in their capacity to form correct judgments;
(*b*) in their powers to carry out plans;
(*c*) in their confidence in their own ability;
(*d*) in their venturesomeness.

Few men possess the qualities required of the entrepreneur to a very high degree, and so entrepreneurs are limited in numbers. It is of great importance, therefore, for any economic system to ensure that men of the required ability be appointed to control businesses if maximum efficiency is to be achieved. Thus, the functions of the entrepreneur are twofold: (a) risk-bearing; (b) managerial.

4. Risk and uncertainty

There are two types of risk:

(a) In some cases statistics can be compiled and the probability of loss can be calculated for an average number of instances. When this is so it is possible to insure against the risk.

(b) The probability of some risks, however, cannot be calculated in this way. Where no two cases are alike statistics of probability cannot be compiled, and so it is not possible to insure against this type of risk. To distinguish risks of this kind from those that are insurable the term "uncertainty" is used.

The business man can insure against most business risks—fire, burglary, etc.—but uncertainty regarding future demand cannot be insured against. The entrepreneur must rely on his own judgment.

Types of uncertainty:

(a) changes in consumers' wants;
(b) changes in consumers' purchasing power;
(c) the amounts of commodities to be supplied by other producers.

5. Reduction of entrepreneurial risk

In a number of ways, however, risk undertaken by an entrepreneur can be reduced:

(a) *Insurance*. It has been seen that many risks are of a type where the probability of occurrence can be calculated and the risk measured. Against these risks it is possible for the business man to insure himself. The principle upon which insurance is based is the *pooling of risks*. A number of people contribute to a fund, out of which payments can be made to those who suffer loss. A comparatively small payment thus secures insurance against a possible heavy loss.

Almost any type of business risk can now be insured against, including, for example, life, goods in transit, fire, theft, accident, sickness, plate-glass, employers' liability, unemployment, weather and, to a limited extent, even bad debts.

(b) *Hedging*. By dealing in *futures* it is possible to eliminate risk due to changes in the prices of raw materials, where their supply is subject to great fluctuations. This is particularly applicable to wheat and cotton. Contracts can be made for the delivery of the commodity at some future date. If, before delivery, prices rise the loss to the buyer is offset by his gain on the futures contract; if prices fall the buyer pays the difference on the futures, his loss on which is balanced by his gain from the fall in price. Hedging is thus a form of insurance against price fluctuations.

(c) *Other means of reducing risk*. Many firms now engage in market research and employ economists and statisticians to study the markets for their products. The increasing volume of statistics relating to economic matters also helps to reduce the entrepreneur's risks. Increased knowledge of markets as a result of these developments makes possible a more accurate forecast of future market conditions.

All these factors help to reduce risk, and in so far as these risks are lessened they cease to be part of the pure entrepreneurial function.

6. The nature of the entrepreneur's work

The sole proprietor undertakes all the functions of the entrepreneur; in the partnership the functions are shared by the partners. The modern limited company permits the separation of the two functions of the entrepreneur, the shareholders bearing the risk and a salaried manager taking control. The shareholders elect the directors, whose main function is to choose officials to undertake the actual running of the business. As a result, ultimate responsibility can be traced back through the directors to the shareholders. Control is chiefly a matter of selecting suitable men capable of making the decisions that will be required of them. In large-scale control a knowledge of men is more important than a knowledge of things. This makes it possible for a capable entrepreneur to move from one industry to another.

QUESTIONS

1. What are the chief functions of the entrepreneur?
2. Explain precisely what is meant by "production". What part is taken by each of the agents in the production of wealth? (R.S.A. Inter.)
3. Examine the circumstances in which dealings in "futures" can be advantageous in either import or export trade. (R.S.A. Adv.)
4. Discuss the following statement: "Enterprise, or risk-bearing, is clearly not a factor of production in the sense in which Land, Labour and Capital are factors of production" (Cairncross). (A.C.A. Inter.)
5. What is the role of the entrepreneur? How is this role affected by the merging of businesses? (I.B.)

VIII. Types of Business Unit

1. The sole proprietor

This is the oldest type of business, and though mostly small, the commonest unit. A single person provides the capital and the entire responsibility falls upon him. He is the entrepreneur.

2. The partnership

An ordinary partnership consists of two or more persons, who share the responsibility and control. The Companies Acts limit the number of partners in a firm to twenty, except in the case of solicitors, accountants, etc. The Limited Partnerships Act 1907, makes possible a "limited" partnership, in which a partner's liability may be limited to the amount he has invested in the business, but such a partner is debarred from assisting in the management of the firm, and there must be at least one general partner. Limited partnerships are rare, the limited company generally being preferred.

3. The limited company

An Act of 1956 extended the principle of limited liability to companies formed for any trading purpose, resulting in the limited joint-stock company becoming the chief form of business organisation in Great Britain. Its chief advantages are:

(a) it can obtain the large amount of capital necessary for large undertakings;

(b) expansion is easy, and can be financed from reserves or by a further issue of shares;

(c) a Board of Directors can embark upon a more ambitious policy than an individual;

(d) limited liability can be enjoyed by all members.

4. Types of company
There are two types of company, both of which can enjoy the advantages of limited liability:

(a) *The private company*. It may have from two to fifty members, but it cannot offer its shares to the general public. A shareholder cannot transfer his shares without the consent of the other shareholders. Where a company is under the control of five or fewer persons or families it is known as a *close company*.

(b) *The public company*. It must have at least seven members. Its shares can be bought and sold on the stock exchange if there is a stock exchange quotation for them. A copy of its balance sheet must be lodged each year with the Registrar of Companies.

In Great Britain private companies greatly outnumber public companies, but the total capital of the public companies is many times as great as that of the private companies.

5. Shares and debentures
The capital of a limited company may consist of several types of shares, which may be in units of £1, 50p, 25p, 20p, 10p, 5p, etc.

(a) *Ordinary shares*. These have no fixed rate of dividend, and take a share of profits only after all other charges have been met. The dividend on these shares fluctuates from very low rates (or even nothing at all in a trade depression) to high rates in periods of boom. Some firms issue two types of ordinary shares, one bearing a fixed rate of dividend, and the other, known as *deferred ordinary*, taking what remains after the dividends on the other shares have been paid.

(b) *Preference shares*. These carry a fixed rate of dividend and are paid in full before any share of profits is allocated to the ordinary shares.

(c) *Cumulative preference shares*. The advantage of these shares is that any arrears of dividend from a previous year are paid before payment is made on the ordinary shares.

(*d*) *Participating preference shares.* These receive a fixed minimum rate of dividend, but they are also entitled to an additional amount if total profit exceeds a prescribed amount.

(*e*) *Debentures.* These are not shares but loans to the company. Debenture holders are therefore creditors of the company, and as such are entitled to the interest on their loans before any profits are distributed among the shareholders.

Table VI shows the method of distribution of profits.

TABLE VI. *Distribution of Profits.*
Capital of Company: £300,000

	Profit	£30,000	£13,000	£7,000
5% Debentures (£100,000)	Interest	5%	5%	5%
6% Preference shares (£100,000)	Dividend	6%	6%	2%
Ordinary shares (£100,000)	,,	19%	2%	Nil

6. The co-operative society

This type of business dates from 1844, when twenty-eight weavers founded a co-operative society at Rochdale. Members may invest up to £1,000 in their societies, but each member is only entitled to one vote. The members elect a president and a committee, which acts like a Board of Directors of a limited company, deciding general policy and appointing paid officials. Profits are distributed among the members in proportion to the value of their purchases. The loyalty of members has had a steadying effect upon the volume of business done.

7. Public enterprise

(*a*) *Operation of local authorities.* At one time, many more commercial services were provided by local authorities than is the case today. Some, however, still supply water and provide passenger transport services. Committees of the local councils are responsible for management and exercise control.

(b) *Operation by the State*. The Post Office is the oldest commercial undertaking in Great Britain operated by the State. In the case of nationalised industries—coal, transport, gas, electricity, etc.—public corporations have been set up to manage them. This type of business unit was developed before 1939, and was the form of organisation adopted, for example, for the B.B.C.

QUESTIONS

1. Write a note on the evolution of the joint-stock company as a type of business organisation. Point out its shortcomings and contrast it with the other types of organisation to be found in this country today. (R.S.A. Adv.)

2. Distinguish between a private and public joint-stock company.

3. Compare a co-operative society and a limited company with regard to (a) organisation, and (b) distribution of profits.

4. Describe carefully the main characteristics of: (a) a limited company, (b) a public corporation. (G.C.E. Ord.)

IX. Problems of the Firm

1. Co-ordination of the factors of production

The Principle of Substitution. After uncertainty bearing, the next important function of the entrepreneur is co-ordinating the factors of production. For some forms of production it may be that the factors must be combined in fixed proportions, but more often it is within the power of the entrepreneur to vary the proportions, employing more of one factor and less of another. A certain minimum amount of each factor is required, but above that it may be possible to substitute capital for labour, or labour for land, etc.

The amount of any factor that the entrepreneur will employ depends upon its price. Factors are scarce relative to the demand for them. Thus factors will tend to be distributed among various industries in such a way that the *marginal productivity* of each is equal. If this were not so it would be advantageous to transfer a factor with a low marginal productivity in one industry to another industry if its marginal productivity would be higher there. When there is no tendency for factors to move, equilibrium is established. Under actual conditions, however, factors are not perfectly mobile.

2. Mobility of factors

A completely specific factor can only be put to one use, and is therefore immobile. Most factors are not completely specific, and the less specific they are, the greater is their mobility. As noted in V, 3, there are two aspects of mobility—occupational and geographical.

(*a*) *Land.* Obviously land is not mobile in the geographical sense, but it can be put to some alternative use, that is, it may be specific or non-specific. Most land can be applied to more than one use—it can be employed as farmland or it can be built upon.

(b) *Labour.* Most people prefer not to move from one country to another, often in spite of such inducements as higher wages; many people are reluctant even to move to another part of their own country, this being particularly noticeable whenever a highly-localised industry declines, so that some parts of Great Britain suffer much more severely from unemployment than others. Nevertheless, during 1920–39 and again after 1945 there was some drift of population from northern to southern England and, more recently, away from London.

Some occupations require a long or expensive period of training, and in this and other ways (e.g. by qualifying examinations) entry to the professions is restricted. For some occupations special aptitude is necessary. On the other hand, there are many occupations that are not difficult to enter. The entry of boys and girls into employment and the retirement of older workers form the main methods by which labour is redistributed among occupations. One of Lord Beveridge's three conditions for the maintenance of Full Employment was that there should be organised mobility of labour.

(c) *Capital.* Much capital is highly specific, but factory buildings and some kinds of machinery are capable of alternative use. Capital, too, though durable, wears out and can then be replaced either by similar or newer types.

3. Advantages of large-scale production
During the past two hundred years there has been a tendency for firms to increase in size. The main motive for expansion has been to increase profit by securing economies associated with large-scale production. Where an individual firm by itself can obtain these economies they are termed internal economies. The chief internal economies of large-scale production are:

(a) *Economy in the use of land.* It is rare for an increase in output to require a proportionate increase in the amount of land employed.

(b) *Greater efficiency of labour.* Greater specialisation

will make it possible for workers to acquire greater skill. The large firm, too, can usually offer a number of better-paid posts on both the administrative and on the technical side, and so it may attract to it men of greater ability.

(c) *Economies in the use of capital.* A more capitalistic method of production will be possible, and so it may enjoy many technical economies. The large firm may be able to use larger units of capital which are usually more economical. Some units of capital are large and indivisible, and cannot be employed to full capacity by small firms. Some plant is too expensive for the small firm.

(d) *Economies of administration.* An increase in output will probably not require a proportionate increase in clerical staff. In a large firm, the manager can delegate much of the control to subordinates and devote himself more to problems of policy and organisation.

(e) *Economy of material.* A large firm has less waste on account of the development of the manufacture of by-products. The waste of a small firm would not be worth dealing with in this way.

(f) *Economies of marketing.* A large firm enjoys economies in both buying and selling; it buys its raw material in bulk at lower prices, and, in proportion to output, its selling costs are lower, especially costs of advertising.

(g) *Financial economies.* The large firm can usually borrow on better terms than the small firm and can raise additional capital more easily.

(h) *Research.* A large firm can set up its own research department, whereas a small firm could not afford this.

(i) *Welfare facilities.* A large firm can give more attention to the welfare of its workers, providing canteens, social and sports clubs, etc. Such facilities tend to increase efficiency.

4. Disadvantages of large-scale production
Large-scale production is not, however, without its drawbacks:

(a) More *organisation* is required, with the consequence that more rules and regulations are necessary.

(*b*) The sole proprietor has more *independence*, and changes in policy and organisation can be introduced without delay or the necessity for consulting others.

(*c*) The *self-interest* of the sole proprietor is an incentive to efficiency. Whether he has more initiative than a hired manager is perhaps open to doubt.

The survival of the small firm. Though the advantages of large-scale production easily outweigh the disadvantages many small firms still survive. Some reasons for the survival of the small firm are where:

(*a*) the optimum size of the firm is small;

(*b*) the technical unit is greater than the managerial and this requires the firm to put out some processes to small firms (*see* page 50);

(*c*) craftsmanship is involved;

(*d*) the market for the commodity is restricted;

(*e*) personal attention can be given, as in the retail trade.

5. Limits to large-scale production

A firm cannot expand indefinitely. Some of the principal checks to expansion are:

(*a*) *The extent of the market.* For some things the total demand is small, and so large-scale production is not possible.

(*b*) *Organisation.* The larger a firm, the more complex becomes its organisation, and the number of entrepreneurs capable of managing very large firms is limited. This is probably the chief limitation on large-scale production.

(*c*) *Increasing cost of factors.* Since factors of production are relatively scarce, entrepreneurs compete for them. The demand for the additional factors necessary to increase the size of the firm will force up their prices, and so increase the cost of production.

(*d*) *Falling price of the commodity.* If a firm expands to such an extent that its output forms an appreciably larger proportion of total production its output may have to be sold at a lower price.

Therefore, as a firm expands its marginal costs after a time tend to rise and marginal revenue tends to fall. The absolute limit to expansion will be the point where marginal revenue and marginal cost are equal, since any further expansion will result in less profit.

6. The location of industry

External economies. A single firm may be able to obtain internal economies by expanding its output. External economies, on the other hand, are outside the control of a single firm, but may be achieved by an industry as a whole. External economies arise from the localisation of an industry—that is, its concentration in a particular district.

Advantages of localisation. From division of labour within a firm it is a short step to division of labour within an industry, that is, regional division of labour, and this is possible where it is concentrated within a small area. The cotton industry of Lancashire (now much reduced) and the woollen industry of West Yorkshire are typical. As a result:

(a) firms are able to specialise in single processes, e.g. spinning, weaving, dyeing;

(b) local skill is developed for the particular industry;

(c) subsidiary industries grow up, e.g. manufacture of textile machinery, manufacture of dyes. Situated close to the basic industry they meet its special need;

(d) organised markets for the local industry may be established.

7. Influences on location of industry

At different periods the location of industry in Great Britain has been influenced by different considerations:

(a) *The period before 1914.* When the older industries of Great Britain were established the chief factors affecting their location were: (i) nearness to power (at first water, later coal), and (ii) proximity to raw materials. As a result a feature of the Industrial Revolution was the drift of population from the South of England to the Midlands and the North, with a concentration of population on the coalfields. Industrial inertia, however, is strong, especially where a great deal of fixed capital has been laid down, and heavy industry particularly tends to remain in certain districts long after the original advantages of its location have passed away.

(b) *Between the two world wars (1919–39).* The development of road transport and a new means of power (electricity) lessened the importance of the earlier influences on location. It became more important to be near to large centres of population as a market. Under these conditions, therefore, a vast conurbation such as London became of itself a magnet for new industries. As a consequence, the earlier drift of population was reversed, and a movement from north to south took place. In a period of ten years between the two world wars the number of insured workers in the London area increased by over 500,000, while the number of such workers in South Wales declined by 176,000, Durham suffering a loss of over 100,000 and South Lancashire a loss of 94,000. The districts losing workers were all "distressed areas".

(c) *The period since 1945—planned location of industry.* There is, however, a serious disadvantage to localisation. If the prosperity of a district is dependent upon one basic industry a fall in the demand for its products affects the entire area—that is, structural unemployment becomes in effect mass unemployment in particular districts. This was the cause of high unemployment in Lancashire in 1950, and in South Wales, Durham and Clydeside in 1962–68, although most of the rest of the country at those times was enjoying full employment.

The second of Lord Beveridge's conditions for the maintenance of full employment was controlled location of industry. The Distribution of Industries Act 1945, was the first step towards planned location of industry. Certain areas with high-localised industries were declared to be development areas, and the aim was to give them greater variety of industries, so that a fall in the demand for the products of one industry would not affect the whole district. To this end new industries were encouraged to set up in these regions. The contraction of the cotton industry made essential the attraction of new industries to Lancashire. It was hoped in this way to check the drift to London and south-east England.

The Local Employment Act 1960, empowered the Government to assist any area in the United Kingdom, known until 1966 as a development district, where unemployment was in excess of the average for the country as a whole. Thus, West Cornwall came to be so designated.

The Industrial Development Act 1966, abolished the development districts, revised the development areas and greatly enlarged their boundaries. Thus, the whole of Scotland, Northern Ireland, Northern England (north of a line from Morecambe Bay to Flamborough Head), Wales, Cornwall and Devon became development areas. Increased grants and investment allowances were to be paid to firms setting up in these areas, together with a premium for each employee.

In 1967 a Regional Employment Premium was introduced, whereby firms in development areas were to receive a grant depending on the number of their employees. The country has been divided into ten economic planning regions. In addition to the development areas some districts have been declared to be Special Development Areas, so that attention can be given to their particular problems. There are also some Intermediate (or "Grey") Areas that have special problems though not severe enough for them to be designated development areas.

New Towns. To check the further expansion of densely populated areas, especially London, some New Towns have been established. Most new towns were planned to have populations up to 100,000 but Milton Keynes in Buckinghamshire and Craigavon in Northern Ireland were planned as new cities, each eventually to have upwards of a quarter of a million inhabitants. Some Government departments have been moved from London. The aim was to develop small industrial centres and not merely residential places. New Towns which have reached a considerable stage of development include Crawley, Harlow, Stevenage, Basildon and Hemel Hempstead in the south, Corby in the Midlands, Newton Aycliffe in the north-east, Cwmbran in South Wales and East Kilbride in Scotland. In addition a number of existing towns of moderate size are being expanded. These include Peterborough, Northampton, Swindon and Aylesbury.

By 1977, however, the loss of industry and population in Inner London was proceeding at such a rapid rate that many people regarded it as excessive and thought it should be checked.

8. The optimum firm

In every industry there is a certain size of firm where the costs of production per unit of output will be lowest. This is the optimum firm. Under perfect competition firms would tend to reach this size. The main problem facing a firm striving to reach the optimum is the difficulty of reconciling the differing optima of the component parts of the firm—the technical, financial, managerial and marketing units. Here are some of the methods by which the technical and managerial optima can be reconciled:

(a) *Where the technical optimum is greater than the managerial:*

(i) Vertical disintegration, i.e. putting out some processes to small firms. This is one reason for the survival of the small firm.

(ii) Setting up a number of productive departments with separate managements and with a central office to co-ordinate them.

(iii) Reduction of the technical unit by concentrating on fewer varieties of the product.

(b) *Where the managerial optimum is greater than the technical:*

(i) By duplication of the technical unit.

(ii) By producing another commodity of similar type or more varieties of the original product.

(iii) By setting up large and small plants, especially where there are seasonal fluctuations in the demand for the product.

9. Diminishing and increasing returns

The Law of Diminishing Returns has already been touched upon in IV **6**. It is usual now to relate the law to the proportions in which the factors of production are combined. Diminishing returns occur if the factors are not combined in the optimum proportion. By employing more labour in proportion to capital, after a point diminishing returns will set in. The difficulty of combining the factors in the best proportion may be due to one of the factors consisting of large and indivisible units. If output is contracted it may still be necessary to employ the whole of this indivisible factor. Similarly, if an increased output can be obtained only by the employment of another large indivisible unit of machinery, which will not be fully employed, then the increased output will be achieved only at the cost of diminishing returns, i.e. increasing costs. Thus the Law of Diminishing Returns is a law of proportions.

Increasing returns to scale (or decreasing costs) occur when the expansion of a firm produces economies and greater efficiency. If a firm is below the optimum size expansion will show increasing returns. Whenever the expansion of a firm results in its being able to enjoy internal economies there will be increasing returns to scale.

10. Costs of production

Expansion of output may, therefore, be achieved under conditions of (a) diminishing returns, (b) increasing returns, or (c) constant returns, i.e. where costs increase proportionately with output.

Fixed and variable costs. Fixed costs are those that do not vary with every change in output, e.g. the cost of plant and management; variable costs vary with output, e.g. labour, raw materials.

(*a*) *Prime costs.* These include all variable costs and some of the fixed costs, e.g. costs of administration. In the short period, a firm may continue in production if it can only just cover its prime costs.

(*b*) *Supplementary costs.* These are the rest of the fixed costs. In the long period a firm must obviously cover both sets of costs.

Selling costs. These costs are incurred in order to develop or widen the market for a commodity. Advertising is the principal selling cost. It has been calculated that advertising accounts for 45% of the costs of production of patent medicines, 35% in the case of patent foods and toilet requisites and 10% for food and household goods.

QUESTIONS

(*i*) *Economies of large-scale production*

1. Distinguish carefully between "internal" and "external" economies and give two illustrations of each. (I.B.)
2. State in summary form the advantages and disadvantages of large- and small-scale production. (C.I.S. Inter.)
3. What do you understand by the "optimum" size of a firm? What are the principal factors which determine it?

(*ii*) *Location of industry*

1. Examine the main factors determining the location or geographic distribution of industry and illustrate your answer from any two widely differing industries. (I.B.)
2. Discuss the main factors that have influenced the localisation of industry in the United Kingdom in the last twenty-five years. (I.C.M.A. Inter.)

3. What do you understand by a "development area"? Give examples and state what measures have been taken by the Government to help these areas. (G.C.E. Ord.)

(iii) Increasing and diminishing returns

1. Give a careful explanation of the laws of diminishing and increasing returns, and examine the extent to which either has been affected by mass production. (G.C.E. Ord.)

2. It is often said that the Law of Diminishing Returns operates predominantly in agriculture and the Law of Increasing Returns in industry. Give reasons for agreeing or disagreeing. (C.I.S. Inter.)

(iv) Mobility of factors, costs, etc.

1. Indicate the main factors tending to restrict the mobility of labour and discuss the possible effects of such restriction upon relative wage-rates in different occupations. (I.B.)

2. Distinguish between prime and supplementary costs and explain the importance of the distinction.

3. What is meant by *mobility* of labour? Why, and how, do governments try to make labour more mobile? (G.C.E. Ord.)

X. Markets

1. What is a market?

The term *market* was originally restricted to mean a particular place where buyers and sellers of goods could meet to do business. The development of transport and other means of communication and banking has made it possible for buyers and sellers to get in touch with one another even though they may be thousands of miles apart. A market, therefore, can be considered as an area, however large or small, where buyers and sellers are in sufficiently close contact with one another for goods to tend to sell at the same price (excluding costs of transport) in all parts of the market. There are still many small markets, especially for perishable goods, but for many commodities the market is now world-wide.

There are markets for all kinds of goods and services—manufactured goods, raw materials, foodstuffs, stocks and shares, foreign currency, etc., and we also speak of a labour market.

2. Perfect markets

In a perfect market similar goods are sold at the same price (with allowance for costs of transport). To achieve this three conditions are necessary:

(a) Buyers and sellers must be immediately aware of what is happening in all parts of the market, so that demand in one part of the market affects prices in all other parts of the market.

(b) There must be a large number of buyers and sellers, each one too small to influence the market.

(c) The commodity must be homogeneous, so that no buyer has a preference for the commodity offered by any particular seller.

3. Imperfect markets

Obviously the conditions necessary for a perfect market do not exist in actual conditions with the result that actual markets are therefore imperfect. This is especially true of retail markets, where the ignorance and inertia of buyers encourage imperfection. Most retail buyers generally prefer not to waste time by seeking out sources of supply where prices may be slightly lower.

4. Highly-organised markets

The markets for many commodities are highly organised. In such cases either buyers and sellers are brought together in the same building, or they are in easy touch with one another by telegraph or telephone. The more highly organised these markets are, the nearer they approach to perfection. They are chiefly wholesale markets for imported foodstuffs and raw materials. The stock exchange is nearly a perfect market. In an organised market business is usually conducted according to a definite set of rules, and differences of procedure are largely due to differences in the types of commodities dealt in. Where goods can be graded there is no need for the commodity to be on view, the goods then being sold by private treaty. In other cases, goods are sampled and then sold by auction. The following are examples of such markets·

(a) *The Liverpool Cotton Exchange.* The commodity is graded by the Liverpool Cotton Association, which consists of merchants, brokers and spinners. This makes possible the sale of goods even before their arrival at port, or even before the crop has been harvested. Thus prices are quoted both for future delivery, i.e. "futures" (*see* above, VII 5(*b*)) and spot, i.e. for immediate delivery. Entry to the exchange is limited to members.

(b) *The London Wool Exchange.* Wool cannot easily be graded, and it is therefore sold by sample. The selling broker warehouses the wool, takes samples of each bale and issues a catalogue. The wool is then sold by auction. Expert wool buyers attend the sales.

(c) *The London Commercial Sales Rooms.* Auctions are

held here for such commodities as tea, coffee, cocoa, sugar, etc. Tea is imported on consignment and stored in bonded warehouses until the import duty has been paid. Samples are tasted by prospective buyers, after which the commodity is sold by auction.

(d) *The Stock Exchange.* This is an almost perfect market owing to: (i) the ease of transfer of the commodity from one person to another; (ii) the close contact by telephone between one exchange and other similar markets in different parts of the world; and (iii) the commodity dealt in being perfectly homogeneous. Only members are allowed to enter the exchange, and business is carried on according to fixed rules. There are two types of members—brokers and jobbers. The jobbers specialise in particular securities, while it is the function of the brokers to act as agents for investors who are not permitted to deal directly with the jobbers. (*See* below, XXV 5–6.)

QUESTIONS

1. What is a market? Give a brief description of the main kinds of market.

2. What conditions must be fulfilled to make a market perfect? What markets under actual conditions approach most nearly to perfection?

3. What is a market? Compare the market for securities with the market for second-hand books. (G.C.E. Ord.)

XI. Supply and demand

1. Demand

By demand is meant not merely desire for a thing but effective demand, i.e. the amount of a commodity that will be bought over a particular range of prices. For most goods more will be bought at a lower than at a higher price. This does not imply a change in demand, but is simply an expression of the behaviour of buyers when their demand is at a particular intensity. Without any change in the intensity of an individual's demand for fish he will buy more when the price is low than when the price is high.

2. Demand schedules

A demand schedule shows the effect of a given intensity of demand on the amount of a commodity that will be bought over a certain range of prices. Each individual has his own demand schedule for each commodity for which he has a demand. The demand schedules of all consumers of cocoa can be combined to form a market demand schedule for cocoa such as shown in Table VII.

TABLE VII. *Demand Schedules of Cocoa.*

Price per tin	Demand per week (No. of tins)
7p	110,000
6½p	119,000
6p	127,000
5½p	134,000
5p	140,000
4½p ←	145,000
4p	149,000

This is a purely hypothetical demand schedule, but it illustrates the principle that at a lower price more of the commodity will be demanded. At the lower prices some people buy more than they did before, and others enter the market as buyers who were previously unwilling to buy when prices were higher. This illustrates the first of the five laws of Supply and Demand. It assumes, however, that no change takes place in the general conditions of demand. It only shows the state of demand at a given time. At a later period the state of demand may change and, if so, a new demand schedule will be required.

3. Demand curves

A market demand schedule can be represented by a graph (Fig. 1).

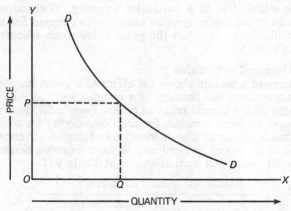

FIG. 1—*A Typical Demand Curve.*

The curve *DD* represents the state of demand at a particular time. *OY* is the price scale and *OX* the quantity scale; from *O* to *X* the quantity of the commodity increases, and from *O* to *Y* the price increases. The dashed lines show that at price *OP* the quantity *OQ* will be demanded. In a similar way the amounts that would be demanded at other prices can be read off from the graph. Since a greater quantity is demanded at a lower price, the demand curve usually slopes downwards. The *First Law* of Supply and Demand, therefore, states that the lower the price of a commodity, the greater the quantity that will be demanded.

Exceptional demand curves. In a few exceptional cases the quantity demanded of a commodity may be greater at a higher than at a lower price:

(a) *Inferior goods.* Some of the cheaper necessary foods, such as bread and potatoes, sometimes show an increase in sales if there is a slight rise in price, and so provide an example of exceptional demand. If at the old price a poor family could afford a certain quantity of these foodstuffs, together with a small quantity of more expensive foods, a rise in the price of these necessaries would perhaps make it impossible to purchase as much as before of the dearer foods, which would be replaced by additional quantities of bread and potatoes. These are sometimes known as Giffen goods.

(b) *Fear of a further increase in price.* This is particularly likely to occur in periods of severe inflation. In these circumstances consumers may buy more of some things even though prices have risen. It also often occurs with stock-exchange securities.

(c) *Articles of ostentation, etc.* These are commodities that are desirable to some people only if they are expensive. Some articles of jewellery are probably of this type. At a higher price more may be bought than at a lower price.

In all these cases the demand curve will slope upwards, but only for a part of its length, for demand could not be expected to continue to increase with every successive rise in price.

4. Inter-related demands

(a) *Joint demand.* Often the demand for two commodities is linked together, e.g. bread and butter, tea and sugar. Such linked commodities are generally demanded in similar proportions, an increased demand for one producing a proportionately increased demand for the other. If a fall in price results from an increased supply of one commodity, then the price of the other, its supply not having increased, will probably rise.

(b) *Derived demand.* Sometimes a change in the demand for one commodity is the result of a change in the demand for another, e.g. cheaper motor cars would probably increase the demand for petrol. This is known as derived demand.

(c) *Competitive demand.* Two commodities may be fairly good substitutes for one another, e.g. butter and margarine, and in this case increased demand for one will reduce the demand for the other and so lower its price.

(d) *Composite demand.* This occurs where a commodity, especially a raw material, serves more than one purpose. Thus, raw wool is the basis for both cloth and carpets, an increased demand for one purpose reducing the amount available for the other.

5. Elasticity of demand

This is the degree of responsiveness of demand to changes in price.

(a) Demand is said to be *elastic* if a slight rise or fall in price produces a considerable change in the amount of the commodity demanded.

(b) Demand is *inelastic* if there is little change in the amount demanded in response to a change in price.

(c) If there is a proportionate change in the amount demanded as a result of a change in price the elasticity of demand is said to be *equal to unity*.

The same demand curve may show different elasticities in different parts of its length (Fig. 2).

The less steep the curve, the more elastic will be the demand, provided that the curves to be compared are drawn to the same price and quantity scales. The demand curve in Fig. 2 shows that at high prices—between OP^2 and OP^3—demand is rather inelastic. At medium prices—between OP^1 and OP^2—demand is fairly elastic.

Over the lowest range of prices—up to OP^1—demand again becomes rather inelastic.

The demand of different groups of people for some goods will have different elasticities, depending largely on differences of income and style of living. In the case of luxury foods, however, the demand of both wealthy and poor people may be inelastic, the wealthy buying it what-

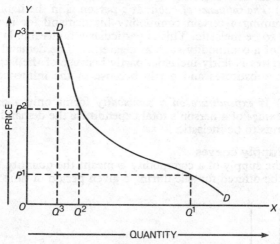

FIG. 2—*Elasticity of Demand.*

ever its price and the poor hardly ever buying it at all; at the same time the demand for this commodity of people of moderate means may be very elastic, a rise in price causing a big decrease in their purchases.

Elasticity of demand depends on:

(a) *The possibility of substitution.* This is the chief determinant of elasticity, whether the goods in demand are luxuries or necessaries. If there are good substitutes for a commodity its demand tends to be elastic, a rise in price causing purchasers to buy the substitute. If there is no good substitute within the same price range demand tends to be inelastic, as for bread.

(b) *The degree of necessity.* This will influence elasticity of demand only if there are no good substitutes for the commodity.

(c) *The incomes of consumers.* The higher a person's income, the more inelastic his demand is likely to be for more expensive goods.

(d) *The influence of habit.* If a person is in the habit of consuming a certain commodity his demand for it will tend to be inelastic. This is particularly noticeable in the case of a commodity such as cigarettes. The demand for cigarettes is fairly inelastic, partly because of the lack of close substitutes and partly because of the influence of habit.

(e) If *expenditure on a commodity* forms only a *small percentage* of a person's total expenditure the demand for it tends to be inelastic.

6. Supply curves

By the supply of a commodity is meant the quantity that will be offered for sale during a given period of time at a

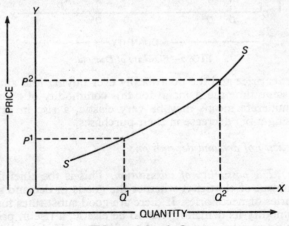

FIG. 3—*A Supply Curve.*

particular price. Generally at a higher price a greater amount will be offered for sale than at a lower price. The reason for this is that all firms do not have equal costs of production, and those with high costs can produce at a profit only when the market price is high. As the market price rises new firms come into production and existing firms increase their output. Thus, the supply curve is related to cost of production.

The *Second Law* of Supply and Demand states that at a high price a greater quantity of a commodity will be supplied than at a low price. Consequently, if a graph is drawn to represent supply the curve usually slopes upward (Fig. 3). This shows that at the lower price OP^1 the smaller quantity OQ^1 will be offered, whereas at the higher price OP^2 the greater quantity OQ^2 will be offered for sale.

If supply were fixed it would be represented by a vertical straight line (Fig. 4).

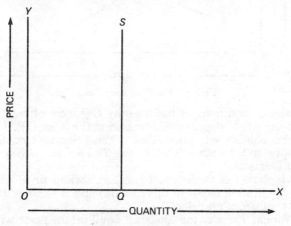

FIG. 4—*Fixed Supply*.

This shows that the supply offered will be the same whatever the price, which will then depend upon the demand for the commodity. In the short period the supply of many goods is often fixed.

7. Equilibrium price

If the conditions of supply and demand for a commodity were capable of calculation it would be possible to plot both curves on the same graph (Fig. 5), and their point of intersection would show the quantity required to satisfy demand at the price shown.

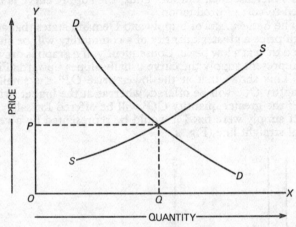

FIG. 5—*The Equilibrium Price.*

In these conditions, if the quantity *OQ* were offered for sale the whole supply could be sold at the price *OP*. This is the equilibrium price, that is the price that equates supply and demand. This is the *Third Law* of Supply and Demand.

Market Price is the short-run equilibrium price when supply is often fixed. In this case demand is the predominant influence on price.

Normal Price is the long-run equilibrium price when supply has had time to adjust itself. In the long run price must cover cost of production.

8. Changes in demand

If demand changes it will be necessary to draw a new demand curve (Fig. 6). An increase in demand means that a greater quantity will be demanded at each price and, therefore, the new curve will be to the right of the old.

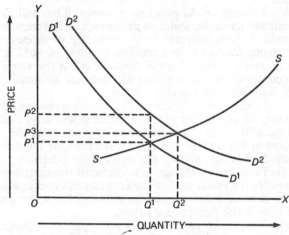

FIG. 6—*Effects of an Increase in Demand.*

The curve D^1D^1 represents demand before the change; D^2D^2 shows demand after the change. Before the change of demand the equilibrium price was OP^1, at which the quantity OQ^1 was supplied. Supply may be slow to adjust itself to a change of price. The immediate effect, therefore, of the increase in demand is for the price to rise from OP^1 to OP^2, supply for a time remaining unchanged at OQ^1. Eventually a new equilibrium price of OP^3 will be established at which the quantity OQ^2 will be demanded.

The *Fourth Law* of Supply and Demand states that an increase in the demand for a commodity will raise its price and increase the quantity supplied.

9. Causes of changes in demand
The following are some of the main causes of changes of demand:

(a) *A change of fashion or taste.* Changes in fashion are often difficult to predict and may take place quite suddenly. Changes in taste are usually much slower to take effect.

(b) *A change in the quantity of money.* This will cause modifications in the scales of preference of different individuals. A 50% increase in the quantity of money will not result, therefore, in a uniform increase of 50% in all prices, since the elasticity of demand is not the same for all commodities. Some prices will increase by more than 50% and some by a smaller amount.

(c) *A change in real income.* This means a change in the quantity of goods that people's incomes will buy. Such a change will affect their demand. An increase in the real income of buyers will increase the demand for some commodities, but may reduce the demand for others.

(d) *Taxation.* A change may occur in the distribution of wealth as a result of changes in taxation. Greater equality of income will increase the demand for some goods but reduce the demand for others.

(e) *Changes in population.* Two types of change of population are possible: (i) a change may occur in the distribution of population between the different age groups, and this will affect demand to the extent that people of different ages have different tastes, thereby causing a fall in demand for some things and an increase in demand for other commodities and services; (ii) a change in the total population, the effect being a general increase or a general fall in demand.

(f) *Expectations of the future trend of business activity.* The demand for producers' goods will vary with the state of trade, increasing enormously in a trade boom, but declining very considerably in a depression.

(g) *Changes in the prices of other goods.* The demand for one commodity may change as a result of a change in the price of another. To some extent all prices are affected in this way, but the connection will be greater for goods that are close substitutes for one another, e.g. butter and margarine.

10. Changes in supply

The following are some reasons why the conditions of supply may change:

(a) *Changes in the technique of production.* This is probably the most important factor affecting supply. The use of a new type of machinery may bring about an increase in output at lower cost.

(b) *Changes in costs of production.* Costs of production must be covered if a firm is to remain in business. A rise in costs, whatever the cause, may result in some firms having to close down, while some others may curtail their output.

(c) *Taxation.* An increase or decrease in the taxation of a commodity, as by value-added tax, is similar to a change in costs of production, and so may affect total supply.

(d) *Effects of the weather.* In the case of agricultural products the weather is an important cause of fluctuations in supply, since output cannot be as accurately estimated in advance as in manufacturing.

The *Fifth Law* of Supply and Demand states that an increase in supply will reduce the price of a commodity and lead to an increase in the quantity demanded.

11. Inter-related supply

(a) *Joint supply.* Commodities that can only be produced together, e.g. wool and mutton, are said to have a joint supply. Often the secondary product is a by-product of the main article of production. The chief problem facing entrepreneurs in such conditions arises when it is desired to increase the supply of one product without increasing the supply of the other. Often, however, the proportion between the two products can be varied, e.g. some sheep produce poor wool and good meat; others produce good wool and poor meat. Generally, however, in such cases, increased demand for one commodity will increase the supply of the other and so reduce its price.

(b) *Competitive supply.* At any given time the output of one good can be expanded only by curtailing the output of another. This is, of course, the basic principle of economics, though it applies more directly in some cases than others. For example, to grow more wheat may mean less grassland for rearing sheep or cattle.

12. The interdependence of demand, supply and price

Demand, supply and price depend on one another. Changes in either supply or demand will affect price. An increase in demand or a decrease in supply will usually raise price; a decrease in demand or an increase in supply will usually cause a fall in price. But these are short-period changes. In the long period an increase in demand will induce an increase in supply, which may eventually cause a fall in price; similarly, if a decrease in demand induces a contraction of supply, the long-period effect may be a rise in price.

Sometimes a change in demand may be offset by a change in supply, so that no change of price takes place, e.g. an increase in the supply of television sets with no change in demand would lower their price, but if at the same time there was a proportionate increase in demand

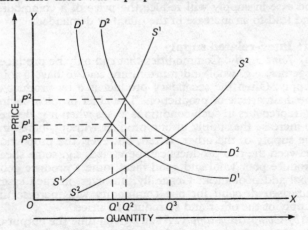

FIG. 7—*Effects of Changes in both Supply and Demand.*

no change in price may occur; a large increase in demand might outweigh the effect of the increased supply, and price might rise.

Therefore, an increase in demand may in the long run bring about an increase in supply. If producers enjoy economies of scale as they expand, production price may eventually fall.

Thus, mass production generally leads to a fall in price (Fig. 7). Before any change took place the equilibrium price was OP^1 at which the quantity OQ^1 was demanded. After the increase in demand the new equilibrium price was OP^2 at which the quantity OQ^2 was demanded. Finally, when supply also had increased a new equilibrium was established at price OP^3 at which the quantity OQ^3 was demanded. Thus, an increase in demand eventually resulted in a lower and not a higher price.

QUESTIONS

1. What determines the price of a manufactured commodity in (a) the short period, and (b) the long period?

2. What are the main causes of (a) changes in demand, and (b) changes in supply?

3. Define elasticity of demand and show whether time is an essential factor in the concept. In what conditions is the demand for a commodity likely to be inelastic? (I.B.)

4. What is the importance in economics of the elasticity of demand? How is it measured? Give illustrations. (C.I.S. Inter.)

5. Examine the effects on the demand for a good of a change in the incomes of consumers. Show how supply may be expected to adapt itself to the new conditions. (G.C.E. Adv.)

6. How far will an increase in the price of beef affect the prices of (a) leather and (b) mutton? Give reasons for your answer. (G.C.E. Ord.)

7. Describe the main economic forces which determine the price of tomatoes. (G.C.E. Ord.)

8. "In the short run, price is determined by demand, and in the long run, by the cost of production." Discuss this statement.

XII. Early Theories of Value

1. The labour theory

According to this theory the value of a commodity depends upon the amount of labour required for its production. The earliest exponent of this view was Adam Smith (1723–90), who said that it was natural that what was the result of two days' labour should have double the value of what was the result of only one day's labour. Ricardo (1772–1823) supported this by saying: "Labour is the foundation of all value". Marx (1818–83) also asserted that the value of a commodity was determined by the quantity of labour expended upon its production.

2. The cost of production theory

This was merely an extension of the labour theory. It was put forward by J. S. Mill (1806–73), who considered that all costs of production, including both labour costs and profit, determined the value of a commodity.

3. Criticisms of early theories

The following are some of the criticisms that have been brought against the early theories of value:

(a) It is difficult to measure the quantity of labour expended upon the production of a commodity. Workers differ in efficiency, and if labour is measured by the time taken to produce a commodity, then a commodity made by an unskilled labourer will have more value than a similar article made by a skilled worker if the unskilled man takes longer to make it, irrespective of the quality of the work. Marx tried to overcome this difficulty by defining the amount of labour by the vague phrase, "socially necessary labour".

(b) Supporters of the labour theory do not make it

clear whether only manual labour is to be taken into account.

(c) Labour may be misdirected. However much labour is put into the making of a useless commodity it cannot have much value.

(d) Goods that have already been produced often change considerably in value, as measured by price, as a result of changes in demand.

(e) These early theories all fail to explain the value of works of art, antiques or other rare things. Clearly the cost of producing a great masterpiece may be much less than the cost of producing inferior work.

(f) Just as the labour of different individuals varies, so the costs of production of firms producing similar goods will vary, and yet the finished products of each firm will probably have to sell at the same price.

(g) But the root cause of the inadequacy of these early theories is that they approach the problem solely from the side of supply and completely ignore the influence of demand.

4. "Scarcity value"

The nineteenth-century economist, Alfred Marshall, though generally accepting the cost of production theory of value, realised its weakness in failing to explain the value of rare commodities. He saw that rare things such as antiques acquired their value from their scarcity.

This, however, did not lead him to build up a complete theory based upon scarcity covering the value of all articles and services. Instead he formulated a dual theory:

(a) to explain the value of commodities the quantity of which can be increased, he considered the Cost of Production theory to be adequate;

(b) the value of commodities that are limited in quantity depends on their scarcity.

QUESTIONS

For questions on Value *see* end of Section XIII.

XIII. The Marginal Utility Theory

1. Utility

In economics, utility is taken to mean the amount of satisfaction to be obtained from goods and services by an individual at a given time. Utility does not depend upon any intrinsic value of a commodity, but upon the consumer's own subjective estimate of the satisfaction that it will yield him at a particular moment. Thus the same commodity will not only have different utilities for different people but also will have different utilities for the same person at different times and in different circumstances. The utility derived from a good cannot, therefore, be measured.

2. Marginal utility

The marginal utility of a commodity is the additional satisfaction derived from having a little more of it.

If, for example, a person who has 15 units of a commodity obtains one more unit, this additional unit is said to be the marginal unit. If, when he had 15 units, he had sold one, the unit thus disposed of would be the marginal unit. Thus the marginal unit is the last to be added or the first to leave a supply.

3. Diminishing marginal utility

The larger a person's supply of a commodity the less utility he derives from an additional unit of it. If he only has a small supply the utility of another unit, i.e. his marginal unit, may be considerable. If, however, he already possesses a fairly large supply of this commodity its marginal utility will be much smaller. Although the units of the commodity are identical, the marginal utility depends upon the size of the consumer's original supply.

For example, a man may be willing to pay 90p for an

extra gallon of petrol if his supply is small. For a second gallon he would perhaps pay only 75p, for a third 60p, for a fourth 40p and for a fifth only 25p. If these prices correctly indicate the utility to him of successive units of this commodity it shows that each additional unit has less utility for him than the preceding one—that is, that marginal utility declines as his stock increases.

4. The origin
Marginal utility, however, begins to decline only after a certain point. A very small quantity of a commodity may be of very little use by itself. The minimum quantity required before a commodity can be of use is known as the origin. In the above example perhaps five gallons of petrol might be the minimum making it worth while to run a car. Only after the car owner had acquired this minimum quantity would the law of diminishing marginal utility begin to operate.

5. Equilibrium distribution of resources
A scale of preferences concerns only the marginal utilities of commodities, and not their total utility. A housewife does not have to decide whether to purchase potatoes or carrots, but whether to have a little more of one and a little less of the other. She will buy just sufficient of each commodity for her estimate of its money-value to equal its price. If she purchases only these two goods the equilibrium distribution of her resources would be achieved when an additional increment of potatoes had less utility for her than the last quantity of carrots, and when an additional increment of carrots had less utility for her than her last increment of potatoes. If this were not so she would obtain more satisfaction by increasing her supply of one commodity and reducing her supply of the other.

The wise disposal of one's resources consists in purchasing just so much of each of a number of goods and services that the marginal utility of each is equal. Thus it is the marginal and not the total utility of a commodity that is important.

6. The significance of costs

Costs of production then have no influence on the value of a commodity once it is offered for sale, since people will only be prepared to pay for it a price which coincides with their estimate of its marginal utility.

Costs have an indirect influence, since they affect supply. Costs have to be incurred in order to obtain the resources required for the manufacture of the commodity, and resources are limited relative to the demand for them. The value put on resources by these competing demands for their use determines the purposes for which they are to be employed. If the price people are prepared to pay is low, resources will be diverted to some alternative use. Costs thus affect price by curtailing or expanding supply.

In the short period, then, value depends on marginal utility alone, but in the long period costs of production have to be met or the commodity will not be produced.

QUESTIONS

1. Is the value of a commodity determined by (a) utility; (b) the amount of labour expended in producing it? (R.S.A. Inter.)

2. Explain the marginal theory of value. (C.I.S. Inter.)

3. "A commodity has value not because labour is put into it: labour is put into it because it has value." Examine this statement, pointing out the forces determining the value of a commodity. (R.S.A. Adv.)

XIV. Monopoly

1. Perfect competition
Under perfect competition it is assumed that production is carried on by a large number of firms, each one of which produces only a small proportion of the total output of the commodity. As a result no single firm can perceptibly influence the total supply, and so cannot influence price by restricting its output. Another condition of perfect competition is that the commodity is homogeneous.

In conditions of perfect competition, therefore, entrepreneurs take it for granted that the price to be obtained for their goods will be the market price. They have thus no incentive to restrict output. Perfect competition, however, is a purely theoretical concept.

2. Monopoly
Absolute monopoly occurs when the entire production of a commodity is in the hands of a single producer. Secondly, there must be no substitute for the commodity. Like perfect competition, therefore, it is a purely theoretical concept. In practice, however, the term is used of any firm, or combination of firms, that produces so large a proportion of the total output of a commodity that it can raise price by restricting output. Even so a monopolist must take account of consumers' demand. He can either (*i*) fix his price and let demand determine his output, or (*ii*) fix his output and let demand determine the price, but he cannot do both of these things.

3. Imperfect competition
Actual conditions lie between the two extremes of perfect competition and monopoly. Thus, there are many forms

of *imperfect* competition, ranging from near-perfection to near-monopoly. Instead of many producers, as in perfect competition, or the single producer of monopoly, there may be only a few producers; instead of a homogeneous commodity there may be differentiation of the product by a device such as a brand name. When production is in the hands of only a few firms it is known as *oligopoly*. In ordinary speech, however, the term monopoly is unfortunately generally used to mean any form of very imperfect competition.

4. Monopoly output

A monopolist will produce that output which will maximise his profits. He will not therefore push his output beyond the stage where marginal cost equals marginal revenue.

Consider Table VIII.

TABLE VIII. *Monopolist Output.*

Units of output	Price per unit	Total revenue	Marginal revenue	Total cost	Marginal cost	Profits
	£	£	£	£	£	£
80	11.00	880	—	733	—	147
90	10.50	945	65	753	20	192
100	10.00	1,000	55	785	32	215
110	**9.50**	**1,045**	**45**	**829**	**44**	**216**
120	9.00	1,080	35	885	56	195
130	8.50	1,105	25	953	68	152
140	8.00	1,120	15	1,033	80	87

A monopolist with an output of 80 units (over a period of time) can sell his total output at £11 per unit, his total revenue, therefore, being £880; and since his total costs are £733, he will obtain a profit of £147.

If he increases his output (over a similar period of time) to 90 units he has to sell at £10.50 per unit. This increases his total revenue by £65, i.e. his marginal revenue is £65. At the same time his costs increase by £20 (his marginal cost). The *marginal revenue* is thus the additional revenue resulting from each successive increase of output. Similarly, *marginal cost* is the additional cost of producing each successive increment of output. In the above example marginal costs are increasing, that is the firm is working under conditions of diminishing returns. Under monopoly marginal cost may be constant, increasing, or decreasing.

The monopolist will go on increasing his output until it reaches 110 units, for at that output his profits reach a maximum—£216. He will have no incentive to increase his output further, for to do so would reduce his profits. At this output marginal revenue and marginal cost are equal (almost, in the example above), and price is greater than marginal cost.

Under perfect competition output would be increased to the point where marginal costs equalled price, so giving a greater output and a lower price than under monopoly. A single firm in perfect competition would have no motive to restrict its output, for it could not appreciably affect total supply by doing so; on account of the large number of producers it must take price as fixed. If the price under perfect competition were £7.50 per unit, to restrict its output to (say) 110 units would yield a total revenue of only £825 with total costs at £829, thus resulting in a loss of £4.

5. Bases of monopoly power

Some degree of monopoly can be obtained in any one of the following ways:

(a) *Where one firm controls a large proportion of total output*, e.g. the Coffee Institute of Brazil.

(b) *Where expensive plant is required*. This tends to keep out new competitors, e.g. in the iron and steel industry. Such a restriction would be effective only in the short period, for if monopoly profits persisted other firms would enter the industry in the long period.

(c) *Where duplication of a service would be wasteful*. In the case of public utilities supplying water, gas, electricity, etc., there is often a large initial expenditure. Duplication would give an inferior service. Before competition from road transport developed, the railways often had monopolies over certain parts of their systems, though competing against one another for long-distance traffic. At one time bus companies competed against one another over the same route, but an Act of 1930 gave them monopolies over certain routes. State undertakings are usually monopolistic. The Post Office has long been a State monopoly. When public companies have been granted monopolies their charges or profits have usually been subject to legal restriction.

(*d*) *Branded goods.* By means of trade marks manufacturers can establish a sort of monopoly. No other firm can use its trade mark and goods so branded are distinct from other goods of a similar type, and by extensive advertising consumers are led to believe that a particular brand is better than other brands. Patent rights have a similar effect.

(*e*) *Local monopolies.* These may arise as a result of: (*i*) ignorance of inertia of consumers; (*ii*) goodwill of a long-established firm; (*iii*) heavy transport costs, e.g. as for coal. Many suburban retail shops enjoy a degree of monopoly on account of their convenient situation.

(*f*) *Tariffs.* These assist monopoly either (*i*) by giving a combine a monopoly in the home market, or (*ii*) by enabling goods to be sold abroad at a lower price than prevails at home. (*See* below, XXVIII 2.)

6. Types of combine
Amalgamations may be of two kinds:

(*a*) *Horizontal*, i.e. where the member firms are all at the same stage of production, e.g. Bradford Dyers' Association, a combine of firms all engaged in dyeing. Cartels are of this type.

(*b*) *Vertical*, i.e. where the members are firms at different stages of production. This type might include firms engaged in transport, coal- and iron-mining, steel production, etc., e.g. the American Steel Trust.

The following are the main types of monopolistic association:

(a) *Cartels*. In its original German form the cartel was a voluntary association of firms whose aim was to keep up the price of their product by limiting output. Voluntary monopoly agreements tend to be unstable and in time break up. When, however, governments are responsible for the schemes they are more likely to be permanent, as in the case of the British agricultural marketing boards for milk, potatoes, hops, eggs, etc. The Government can compel all producers of a farming product to form a cartel if most producers favour one.

(b) *Trusts*. Unlike the cartel, the trust is a complete and permanent amalgamation of firms, generally a particularly large combine. It is of American origin, some of the American trusts being exceptionally large and usually vertical in structure. When a trust is formed the constituent firms completely lose their identity.

(c) *The holding company*. This is the modern method of bringing a group of firms under the same control, and this type of company is to be found in both Great Britain and the United States. It is a purely financial organisation which uses its capital to acquire controlling interests in other companies by purchasing over 50% of their ordinary shares. Companies controlled in this way may have their own subsidiaries, controlled in similar fashion. The great advantage of the holding company is that the companies under its control retain their original names and the goodwill which these names carry. Thus, this type of organisation can hide its real size from the general public, most of whom are quite unaware that apparently rival products are manufactured by firms in association with one another. Examples of holding companies are Unilever Ltd., Vickers Ltd., the United Drapery Trust Ltd., General Universal Stores Ltd.

The most serious drawback to the holding company is that it makes possible a practice known as "pyramiding". This occurs if one man obtains a controlling interest in a holding company, since this gives him complete control of the whole group, even though he may own only a relatively small fraction of the total capital.

7. Discriminating monopoly

Discriminating monopoly occurs when goods or services cannot be transferred from one market to another, with the result that different prices can be charged to different groups of consumers. Discriminating monopoly is thus possible only when the markets can be kept separate. It is profitable for the monopolist to charge discriminating prices only when elasticity of demand is not the same in each market. Markets are most easily separated where personal services are involved, since such services cannot be resold. A foreign market can be separated from the home market by means of tariffs. A few examples of discriminating monopoly follow:

(a) *Doctors.* It used to be customary for doctors to make higher charges for their services to wealthier patients than to poorer people. Clearly, in such a case no one can buy in the cheaper market and resell in the dearer one.

(b) *Transport* (i) *Railways.* Excursions are frequently run by railways at fares less than those ordinarily charged. The railways, too, charge higher rates for carrying more valuable freight than for cheaper, bulky goods. Railways can run a cheap excursion only if most of the passengers carried would otherwise not have travelled. Goods can easily be classified in different categories, and so these markets can easily be kept separate. Thus, "charging what the traffic will bear" is an example of discriminating monopoly. (ii) *Airlines.* By offering special fares airlines too attempt to attract passengers who would not otherwise travel by air. Various kinds of restrictions are imposed to reduce the availability of such fares to ordinary passengers who in any case would be willing to pay the full fare.

(c) *Dumping.* The output figures in Table VIII above show that the monopolist earns his maximum profit with an output of 110 units. To increase his output to 120 would decrease his profit, but if his home market is protected by a tariff he could sell abroad his additional 10 units at a lower price than he charged in the home market, e.g. £6 per unit abroad and £9.50 per unit at home. By doing this he would increase his total profit.

(*d*) *Gas and electricity supplies.* It is possible to discriminate in favour of large consumers of gas and electricity by charging lower rates after a certain amount has been consumed. Lower charges may be offered to consumers who restrict their consumption to off-peak periods. In the case of public utilities fixed costs are usually considerably greater than variable costs. Public utilities tend to charge discriminating prices because they require a large amount of fixed capital whether their output is large or small. Where fixed costs are very great in comparison with variable costs it sometimes leads to the adoption of a two-part tariff system of charging (*i*) a fixed minimum charge to cover fixed costs, and (*ii*) a charge varying with consumption to cover variable costs.

(*e*) *Special editions.* Books are often issued in successively cheaper editions, the various markets in this case being separated from one another by time.

8. Advantages of monopoly
In favour of monopoly it can be said that:

(*a*) monopoly makes possible the planning of production in order to try to equate supply and demand. Planned production results in greater stability of trade, with a consequent reduction of risk;

(*b*) costs can be reduced by the elimination of excess capacity. Redundant works can be closed and other plants then work at full capacity, instead of all working below capacity;

(*c*) competition would be wasteful in the case of public utilities such as electricity as it would require unnecessary duplication of plant and cables;

(*d*) sometimes a more economical distribution of the product becomes possible. For example, in competitive conditions several different milk roundsmen may serve the same street.

If monopoly results in a reduction of costs of production a reduction in price also becomes possible.

9. Disadvantages of monopoly
Monopoly is generally disadvantageous to consumers:

(a) The assortment of goods produced is not that desired by consumers.

(b) Output is generally restricted in order to keep up prices. Consumers, therefore, have to pay higher prices for the smaller quantity of goods put on the market.

(c) Even if monopoly is more efficient than competition, it is not certain that consumers will benefit from lower prices. It is more likely that prices will be higher even when legally controlled and they may therefore have less freedom of choice.

(d) The existence of monopoly often tends to retard the introduction of new methods or new inventions. Competition is an incentive to firms to adopt new and improved methods of production.

10. The control of monopoly power
One of the most difficult problems facing the modern industrial state is the control of monopoly power. Factory Acts, social legislation, the activities of trade unions have prevented the exploitation of labour; Company Law has been expanded to regulate the activities of joint-stock companies; but only recently has anything been done to prevent the exploitation of the consumer. Never for long have consumers succeeded in organising themselves to protect their interests. In recent times, however, governments have taken action against monopolies and fear of government intervention has often curbed monopolists.

Various methods have been employed in order to attempt to control monopoly power:

(a) *By legal action against monopolistic combines*. As long ago as 1890 the United States Government passed an anti-Trust Act outlawing monopolistic trusts. Under this Act the Standard Oil Company was broken up into a number of smaller units. In spite of the American Government's anxiety to check monopoly, it has found great difficulty in doing so. More recently the American courts have checked many of the more undesirable monopolistic practices.

In Great Britain, the Monopolies and Restrictive Practices Act of 1949 set up a Commission to inquire into the manufacture of commodities where production of more than 30% of total output was in the hands of one firm or an associated group of firms, though the Fair Trading Act 1973, defined a monopolist as a producer of 25% of the total output of a commodity. Since it was set up the Commission has inquired into the production of matches, electric lamps, motor-car tyres, cigarettes and tobacco, wallpaper, household detergents and many other commodities, the result of each inquiry being embodied in a published report. In many cases it was reported that producers had not been taking undue advantage of their monopolistic position.

The Restrictive Trade Practices Act of 1956 stated that all existing trade agreements between producers should be investigated to decide whether they were in the public interest. As a result, some agreements were dissolved. This Act legalised resale price maintenance in the case of individual firms, but prohibited concerted action by groups of firms against a retailer who might sell at a price below that fixed by the manufacturer. Resale price maintenance was abolished by the Resale Prices Act of 1964. Then in 1965 came the Monopolies and Mergers Act, which empowered the Board of Trade to inquire into proposed mergers and refer them to the Monopolies Commission if monopoly was suspected.

In 1973, the Monopolies Commission became the Monopolies and Mergers Commission. At the same time, an Office of Fair Trading was set up to protect consumers' interests.

(b) *By legal control.* When it has been recognised that competition would be wasteful monopolies have been granted but only subject to some measure of control, such as legal restrictions on charges, or making increases in distributed profits conditional on reduction of charges. Railway rates in Great Britain have always been subject to public control. Throughout the later nineteenth century the British Parliament was keenly watchful of the railways, and there was progressive intensification of control. In 1931, fares charged by road passenger operators have been subject to sanction by Regional Traffic Commissioners.

(c) *By a State lease of the undertaking.* In France the State undertook the construction of the bed, bridges and stations of the railways of that country and then leased them to the operating companies, which provided the track and the rolling stock.

(d) *By public ownership.* It is presumed that if an industry is operated by a public body such as the State or a local authority it will not take advantage of its monopolistic position to exploit consumers. Local authorities first entered the industrial sphere as operators of public utilities. The State has operated the Post Office since the seventeenth century. Since 1946 many British industries have been nationalised including the Bank of England, the coal-mining and iron and steel industries, railways, waterways, road-passenger transport, electricity and gas production.

(e) *Taxation.* It has been suggested that a special tax should be imposed on monopolists, but this idea has so far proved to be impracticable.

QUESTIONS

1. Set out the several types of capitalistic combination or consolidation of business units. What are: (a) the advantages; (b) the possible dangers of each type to (i) the business concerns themselves, (ii) the purchasing public? (R.S.A. Adv.)

2. Submit a brief discussion of agreements for (a) regulating prices; (b) restricting output; (c) dividing the market. (I.B.)

3. What is the influence (a) of perfect competition, and (b) of imperfect competition, upon the size of a firm and upon its efficiency? (C.I.S. Inter.)

4. "Even a monopolist is subject to the sovereignty of the consumer." Discuss this statement.

5. Examine the limits to the exercise of monopoly power. (G.C.E. Adv.)

6. Outline, with examples, the main factors which encourage the growth of monopoly. (G.C.E. Adv.)

XV. Distribution: (i) Rent

1. The distribution of the national income

The factors of production are combined by entrepreneurs in a certain proportion and then used for productive purposes. Payments are made to the factors of production for their shares in the work of production, these being known as rent, wages, interest and profits. The study of what determines the shares of the four factors in the national income forms the branch of economics known as distribution.

The income accruing to any factor of production is its price—the price to be paid for its services. Prices are determined in a market—in this case, therefore, the factor market. Thus the prices of factors of production depend upon: (a) their relative scarcity; and (b) the alternative demands for their use, i.e. on the forces of supply and demand. There are many competing demands for factors in different industries, the demand for factors being derived from the demand for the commodities they help to produce. The marginal theory of distribution asserts that the price of any factor depends upon its marginal productivity.

2. Ricardo's theory of rent

Ricardo considered that land at the margin of cultivation, i.e. land that was only just worth cultivating, yielded no rent. A piece of more fertile land would yield a greater return, and its excess yield over that of "no rent" land was its rent. Thus, according to Ricardo, rent arose from the natural variation in the fertility of land. For example, if the value of the crop from a given area of the poorest land in cultivation was £3, and the value of the crop from a similar area of more fertile land was £5, the rent of the more fertile land would be £2. Farmers would have to pay more for the use of the more fertile land, and so the net return on land of all grades of fertility would tend to be equal. For, in the above illustration, the farmer using the more fertile land would have to pay £2 more to the owner of the land than the farmer using the inferior land.

3. Criticism of Ricardo's theory

The main defects of Ricardo's theory are to be found in its incompleteness:

(a) he restricted rent to land;

(b) he implied that there would be no rent if all land were of equal fertility;

(c) he ignored the possibility that there were alternative uses for the same pieces of land;

(d) he considered marginal land to be the poorest in cultivation, whereas it may be that a piece of the most fertile land would be the first to cease being cultivated if a fall in the price of the product brought about a contraction of its supply, or if there was an alternative and more profitable use for it;

(e) he based his theory simply on the natural variation in the productivity of land.

4. The modern theory of rent

In the ordinary sense rent is simply a price paid for the use of land, buildings or some other form of property belonging to another person. Economic rent, however, can apply to any factor of production. It is regarded as a surplus accruing to any specific factor, the supply of which is fixed—at least, in the short run—as a result of an increase in the demand for it. Thus, it is a payment received by a factor over and above what was necessary to induce that factor to enter its present employment or to keep it there. It is possible, therefore, to find an element of economic rent in the ordinary payment for land, in wages, in interest and in profit. The most specific land is probably a site in a city centre. An increase in the demand for such sites clearly cannot be matched by an increase in supply, and so an additional payment—an economic rent—has to be paid for the use of such land.

5. Transfer earnings

The amount that any factor could earn in its best-paid alternative use is its transfer earnings. Any excess over this amount, i.e. the price that has to be paid to retain it in its present use, is really a sort of rent. For example, a piece of fertile land on the coast may be worth £500 as wheatland, but if such a piece of land provided an excellent site for a first-class hotel it might be worth £4,000. In that case the difference in its earnings as an hotel site (£4,000) and its transfer earnings (£500) is its rent, namely £3,500.

6. Quasi-rent

For economic rent earned by factors other than land the term "quasi-rent" is sometimes used, though it is not usual now to make this distinction. In the short period the supply of a specific factor often cannot be easily increased. In such a case a sudden increase in the demand for it will enable the factor to obtain an additional payment owing to its relative scarcity. This is a rent or quasi-rent. Since, however, the supply of most factors can in the long run be increased, quasi-rents eventually tend to disappear. Some examples of economic rent follow:

(a) *Economic rent in wages.* An increased demand for any form of specific labour, where a long period of training is required, is likely to give rise to an economic rent, since it will be impossible to increase the supply of such labour in the short run. For some occupations special aptitude is required, as with artists, actors, musicians, etc., and so an increase in their popularity may lead to very high payments being offered for their services. Such payments include a high proportion of rent.

(b) *Economic rent in interest on capital.* This may occur in the case of large, expensive units of capital the supply of which cannot be quickly increased.

(c) *Economic rent in profit.* The surplus profit of a monopolist is really of the nature of a rent, though the scarcity of the product has in this case been contrived by the monopolist himself.

7. Social implications

Since rent is a surplus in excess of what is required to keep a factor in its present employment, it can be regarded as unearned. It has therefore been suggested that rents form an admirable basis for taxation. Proposals have been made at various times that rises in site values of land should be taxed. If, however, economic rent is to be taxed, it should not be limited to rent accruing to land, other factors receiving rent should also be taxed, but these rents are not so easily detected as that accruing to land.

QUESTIONS

1. What is the meaning of the term "rent" in economic theory? (R.S.A. Inter.)

2. Explain the element of rent in wages, interest and profits. (I.B.)

3. What do you mean by quasi-rent? In what respects does it (a) resemble, (b) differ from, economic rent? (I.B.)

4. "Rent is a surplus, not a cost." Explain the meaning of this statement in regard to (a) agricultural land, and (b) urban shops. (C.I.S. Inter.)

5. What factors affect the amount of rent paid for land in (a) rural areas, (b) the great shopping centres of large cities? (G.C.E. Adv.)

XVI. Distribution: (ii) Wages

1. Real and nominal wages
By nominal wages is meant the value of the wages in terms of money—sometimes called money wages. By real wages is meant wages in terms of goods and services the money wages will buy. Thus, nominal wages may be rising, while at the same time real wages are falling, if prices are rising more rapidly than nominal wages.

2. The subsistence theory of wages
This is the so-called "iron law" of wages and is of French origin. It asserts that if wages rise above subsistence level an increase in population inevitably follows, and this again forces wages down to subsistence level. This was probably true at the time the theory was formulated, since a poor harvest in those days meant that many people actually died of starvation. It may still be true of some of the more densely-populated countries where the standard of living is low. During the nineteenth century, however, in spite of the rapid increase of population in England real wages more than doubled during that period.

3. The wages fund theory
This theory was refined by J. S. Mill. Since the productive process takes time, wages have to be paid during the interval from the accumulated stores of past production. Thus, it was thought that there is a sort of fund from which wages are paid, and that the size of this fund forms a limit to the total that can be expended in wages at any particular time. Wages, therefore, depend upon the relation between the size of the working population and the wages fund. It follows therefore that if both the population and the wages fund remain unchanged wages can

rise in one industry only at the expense of wages in other occupations. The theory possibly contains some element of truth. Though there is no such thing as a wages fund, there is no doubt that labour gains by an increase in the accumulated stock of real capital. Also in conditions of full employment because the size of the real national income sets a limit to the total of all incomes, one group of workers can increase their *real* income only at the expense of others.

4. The marginal productivity theory of wages

The marginal product of a factor is the value of the addition to total output from the employment of an extra unit of it. The marginal product of labour, therefore, is the additional income to the entrepreneur resulting from the sale of the extra product following the employment of one more man or, alternatively, the decline in the entrepreneur's income from the reduction of output following the dismissal of one man.

Under perfect competition wages tend to equal the marginal product of labour, for the entrepreneur would increase the amount of labour he employs if wages fell below the value of the marginal product until a position of equilibrium was reached where wages and the value of the marginal product were equal. If, however, wages were higher than the value of the marginal product he would employ less labour in order to raise its marginal productivity. The greater the amount of labour employed relatively to other factors, the lower will be its marginal product. Thus, under perfect competition, according to this theory, it is possible to employ the entire labour force at any time, but only at a wage equal to the value of its marginal product.

5. The market theory of wages

Wages are the price of labour and, like other prices, are determined in a market. There is clearly a supply of labour, and the demand for labour comes from entrepreneurs. If labour was perfectly mobile in both senses of the term there would be a single labour market in which the equilibrium wage would occur when supply was equal to demand, so that wages would be the same in all occupations.

However, there is not a single market for labour. Each type of specific labour has its own separate market, and in addition there is another and much larger market for non-specific labour. In each market there are different conditions both of supply and demand, and therefore different equilibrium prices for labour. Nevertheless, the various labour markets are not entirely separate from one another. Higher wages in some occupations will attract labour from other occupations, this being the method by which expanding industries increase their labour supply at the expense of declining industries. Movement between highly-specific occupations is more difficult, but high wages in one profession will probably result in more school-leavers deciding to train for it.

The main reasons for differences in wages are the factors that tend to reduce the supply of a particular type of labour in relation to the demand for it. The following influences limit supply:

(a) the length of the period of training—in some cases several years at a university;

(b) the necessity of passing a number of prescribed examinations;

(c) some kinds of work can be performed only by people with certain special aptitudes;

(d) some work is disagreeable, dirty, unpleasant or dangerous, often such work is poorly paid because it requires no special skill, and so the supply of labour available for it is large. In recent times, however, disagreeable work has tended to be better paid.

(e) non-monetary advantages of an occupation—pleasant conditions, prestige attached to the job, security of employment—tend to increase the supply of labour in relation to the demand for it and so keep down wages in such occupations.

6. The bargaining theory of wages

The increasing power of the trade unions has led some writers to believe the earlier theories of wages to be inadequate. Supporters of the bargaining theory of wages believe that the level of wages depends on the bargaining strength of the trade union concerned, differences in wages, therefore, being the result of differences in the strength of the respective trade unions. The strength of a trade union depends on (*i*) the size of its membership and (*ii*) the extent of the inconvenience it can cause to the community in the event of a strike.

However, the strength of trade unions lies less in their power to dislocate the economy by means of strikes than in (*a*) the general economic conditions of the time, and (*b*) whether the industry concerned is at the time expanding or contracting. In a trade depression conditions are unfavourable to trade unions, whereas in a trade boom the reverse is true. A prolonged period of full employment is favourable to trade unions, since (*a*) there is likely to be a shortage of labour in some areas, and (*b*) employers can generally cover the wage increases by raising the prices of their products, and so may oppose less vigorously the demands for wage increases. Workers in an expanding industry will suffer less in a depression and gain more in a boom than workers in a union representing a declining industry. Thus, the bargaining theory of wages is ultimately dependent on the forces of supply and demand.

How far, then, can trade unions permanently raise the level of wages of their members? According to the marginal productivity theory, the employer cannot permanently pay wages in excess of the value of the marginal product of labour. If, however, employers have taken advantage of their stronger bargaining position to pay wages below this level, then organised action by a trade union may result in raising wages up to this amount. If a higher wage than this is secured it can only be maintained by increasing the marginal product of labour, either (*i*) by increasing the efficiency of the workers, or (*ii*) by reducing the amount of labour employed.

It has been argued that theories of wages are based on the assumption of perfect competition, so that trade unionism, making for imperfect competition, invalidates the theory. This is not so, for the forces that determine wages under perfect competition also affect wages under imperfect competition, and collective bargaining does not alter this fundamental fact.

In an inflationary period such as 1972–74, money wages may increase in spite of rising unemployment. In the last resort, however, *real* wages depend on the size of the *real* national income. Trade union action may raise money wages, but real wages can be increased only if there is an increase in the volume of production.

High wages may result in increased efficiency, e.g. by improving the physique of the workers. Two other results are possible: (*i*) high wages may stimulate the invention of labour-saving machinery; (*ii*) higher wages in one occupation may attract workers from other industries.

7. Wage-rates
There are different methods of calculating wages:

(*a*) *Standard rates*. These are an advantage to both employers and employees. To the employer the payment of a standard wage saves time and trouble entailed by individual bargaining with each employee. It also makes easier the calculation of labour costs. To the employee it makes possible collective bargaining through his trade union.

(*b*) *Piece-rates and time-rates*. In the case of time-rates a worker receives a certain sum per hour; with piece-rates he obtains a certain sum for a given output. Time-rates are in operation where the work is of a continuous nature, or where the quality of the work is important, or where the work cannot easily be standardised and measured, e.g. bus-driving, shopkeeping, farming. The chief points for and against each system are:

Piece-rates—

(*i*) the quicker or more efficient workers can earn more than the slower or less efficient;

(*ii*) output is probably increased;

(*iii*) costs of supervision are reduced; but—

(*iv*) speed may result in work of poor quality, and so "passers" are required to check each worker's output. Mass-production methods, however, leave the workers little control over quality;

(*v*) it often used to be difficult to fix the rate of remuneration fairly where the work varied in difficulty;

(*vi*) if the earnings of the workers increased there used to be a tendency for the rate per piece to be reduced;

(*vii*) the more careful workers are penalised for taking longer time over their work;

(*viii*) costing is easier;

(*ix*) the attempt to secure high earnings may result in overstrain.

Time-rates—

(*i*) this system is to the disadvantage of the quicker and more efficient workers, who only receive the same rate of pay as the slower and less-efficient workers;

(*ii*) there is less administrative work than for piece-rates;

(*iii*) careful supervision is necessary to prevent slacking.

(*c*) *Profit-sharing schemes.* To give the workers an incentive to expand a firm's output, profit-sharing and co-partnership schemes of various kinds have been tried. Employees have sometimes been encouraged to take up shares in the business, or a proportion of profits may be set aside for distribution in the form of a bonus.

(*d*) *Wages and the cost of living.* A rise in prices is generally regarded as a reasonable ground for a claim for higher wages. Some arguments against this system are:

(*i*) Price changes do not uniformly affect all kinds of labour.

(*ii*) It tends to stabilise real wages instead of allowing for a gradual rise in the standard of living, which improved production should bring about.

(*e*) *Wage drift*. Actual earnings are often considerably in excess of wage-rates on account of additional payments, (known as wage drift), such as overtime or bonuses and various kinds of "fringe" benefits.

8. Effect of inventions

The effect of a new invention upon employment and wages depends upon whether it is of a labour-saving or capital-saving type. If it is a labour-saving invention it will reduce the demand for labour but raise the productivity of the labour employed, and so make possible a rise in wages. In the short run, however, there may be some structural unemployment.

9. Earnings of women

For a number of reasons women in the past were generally paid less than men:

(*a*) Some employers preferred men to women, thinking that men were more reliable.

(*b*) Some kinds of work are not capable of being performed by women.

(*c*) Many women who work, especially married women, are not dependent on their own earnings. In the past this often made them prepared to accept lower wages than men received.

(*d*) Many employers did not consider it worth while to train women for more responsible positions on account of the probability of their leaving to marry.

(*e*) Trade union organisation among women was weaker than among men.

Report of the Royal Commission on Equal Pay (*1946*). The *Majority Report* of this commission ascribed the difference in the earnings of men and women mainly to the greater physical strength and greater efficiency of men. The *Minority Report* affirmed that women were equally as efficient as men, except where physical strength was required.

In many professions there has always been equal pay

for men and women. In 1960 the principle of equal pay for men and women was accepted by the Civil Service and in the teaching profession.

The principle of equal pay for equal work is now generally accepted in the more economically-advanced countries. This principle was supported by the Treaty of Rome (1957), which set up the European Economic Community (*see* p. 169). Both the Treaty of Rome and the International Labour Office of the United Nations at Geneva, however, found difficulty in precisely defining equal work. The ILO tried to resolve the problem by using the term "work of equal value". There is often no basis of comparison as the work done by men and women is frequently totally different in character.

The Sex Discrimination Act (1975). This Act made unlawful discrimination against *either* men *or* women, not only in the case of industrial employment but also in other forms of activity.

QUESTIONS

1. Distinguish between nominal and real wages. Why do rates of wages differ among different occupations? (R.S.A. Inter.)

2. State briefly the various methods commonly used for the remuneration of labour. (C.I.S. Inter.)

3. What are the advantages of piece-work payments over time-rates of wages? Why are time-rates necessary in many occupations? (R.S.A. Adv.)

4. How would you account for differences, in the short and long periods, between wages paid in different occupations? (I.B.)

5. Should wage-rates, in your opinion, vary with changes in the cost of living? (I.C.M.A. Inter.)

6. Give reasons why an architect usually receives a higher income than a bricklayer. What factors have reduced the difference between their standards of living in recent years? (G.C.E. Ord.)

XVII. Distribution: (iii) Interest

1. The payment of interest

The medieval Church opposed the payment of interest on loans because it was thought to be immoral for the lender, generally a rich man, to receive back more than he had lent to the borrower, usually either a poor man or one who had suffered misfortune.

Interest can be considered as a payment made to capital for its share in production, that is, it is the price paid for the use of capital. The element of "waiting" was noticed in connection with capital (*see* VI); interest, therefore, can be regarded as the reward for "waiting". Since capital is scarce relative to the demand for it, interest decides how the available supply of capital shall be distributed among the various industries competing for it. Interest makes possible capitalistic or roundabout methods of production. In practice, however, it is often difficult to distinguish between interest and profit.

Elements of interest. Three elements of interest may be distinguished:

  (a) a payment for risk;
  (b) a payment for the trouble involved;
  (c) a payment for the use of the money (pure interest).

2. The rate of interest

Borrowing and lending are indispensable to the working of a modern economic system. The chief borrowers are the Government, local authorities, nationalised and limited companies. The chief lenders are the banks, finance companies and insurance companies.

The rate of interest is important because:

(*a*) It affects *the development of new businesses* and the expansion of older firms, a low rate encouraging expansion and a high rate checking it. If a new machine cost £1,000 and the rate of interest were 10% it would be unprofitable to borrow at this rate unless the additional net income from its use exceeded £100 per annum.

(*b*) It affects the *rate of saving*. Generally more will be saved the higher the rate of interest. Some saving, however, appears to be independent of the rate of interest. The saving of the rich is often simply the surplus left after they have spent all they wish, but even for them a very low rate of interest may lead to increased spending. Some people may save for a particular purpose, e.g. old age or the education of children, and since a definite sum of money is required a fall in the rate of interest may actually stimulate increased saving. But less than 20% of total saving is by individuals, the remainder coming from the undistributed profits of limited companies.

3. Determination of the rate of interest
A number of theories have been put forward to explain how the rate of interest is determined. The rate of interest can be regarded as the price of loans and determined, therefore, by the forces of supply and demand—the supply of loanable funds in relation to the demand to borrow.

If demand were high relative to supply one would expect a high rate of interest, and if supply were greater than demand a low rate. According to this view, the rate of interest equates the supply of loanable funds with the demand for loans. The supply of loanable funds depends on the time preference of lenders (those who prefer a larger sum in the future to a smaller sum in the present) in relation to the time-preference of borrowers, who prefer present to future spending.

4. Liquidity-preference
The view that the rate of interest equates the demand for loans with the supply of loanable funds is too simple. The fact that banks can create credit complicates the situation. The liquidity-preference theory of interest ex-

plains the rate of interest in terms of people's keenness or otherwise to hold money in liquid form in preference to other assets. This keenness determines people's liquidity-preference. To hold money in liquid form involves a loss of interest, but it will be profitable to postpone investment if it is expected that the rate of yield on stocks is likely to rise. Liquidity-preference, too, is an important influence on the value of money (see XX).

Lord Keynes, therefore, considered the rate of interest to be the "reward for parting with liquidity for a period".

It is theoretically conceivable that the rate of interest could fall to zero, but only if a country's productive power had reached its limit, every industry being equipped to the maximum with the most efficient forms of capital. So long as technique is capable of improvement there will be a demand for new capital. A rising standard of living, too, will provide new openings for the profitable employment of capital. So long as there are many competing demands for capital the rate of interest will remain high.

5. The rate of yield

The prevailing rate of interest is shown by the rate of yield on existing investments. If new 8% stock is issued at par, then £100 of such stock will yield interest of £8 per year. If the stock remains at par on the stock exchange the rate of interest and the rate of yield will remain the same, viz. 8%. If, however, the market value of the stock fell to £80 the rate of interest would still be 8%, but the rate of yield would then be £8 on £80, i.e. 10%; if the market value of the stock increased to £120 the rate of yield would fall to $6\frac{2}{3}$%.

6. Long- and short-term rates

Short-term securities consist of trade bills and Treasury bills, both types usually falling due in three months. Long-term securities consist of stocks with a fixed rate of interest, but on which the rate of yield varies as the market value rises or falls. The long-term rate of interest is usually higher than the short-term on account of the greater risk of a change in the rate of yield of securities over a longer period.

It is largely as a result of the actions of speculators that the two rates of interest tend to follow one another up and down. If the price of stocks rise speculators sell their holdings of these and buy bills; if the prices of stocks fall they sell bills and buy stocks. The fundamental rate is the short-term rate, and it is changes in this that affect long rate. However, if the prevailing rate of interest is very high, the short-term rate may be temporarily higher than the long-term rate.

QUESTIONS

1. What is the importance of the rate of interest? What influences determine the rate of interest and cause the rate to vary from time to time?

2. What is gross interest? Distinguish its component parts. (C.I.S. Inter.)

3. How would you account for the differences (*a*) between the interest paid upon a short loan and a long-term loan, and (*b*) between the interest upon a government loan and an industrial (debenture) loan? (I.B.)

4. (*a*) Distinguish between modern views of Interest and the medieval view of Usury. (*b*) How do economists justify Interest? (A.C.A. Inter.)

XVIII. Distribution: (iv) Profit

1. Elements of profit
Profit forms the remuneration of the entrepreneur. Three elements of profit can be distinguished:

    (*a*) wages of management;
    (*b*) interest on capital;
    (*c*) reward for taking risks.

2. Pure profit
Under static conditions the entrepreneur would receive wages of management and interest, but the third element of profit would tend to disappear, that is, there would be no pure or economic profit, which arises only under dynamic conditions. The classical economists wrote at a time when industry was in an early stage of development, the business firm being small, and the man who provided the capital also managing the business and accepting all the risks of production. Such a man would not distinguish between the various elements of profit, but would regard the whole of his net income from his business as profit.

It has already been noted (*see* VII) that the main function of the entrepreneur is risk and uncertainty bearing. Most business risks can be insured against, except the uncertainty that the entrepreneur has to bear. Dynamic (that is, changing) conditions make for uncertainty about the future. The entrepreneur's reward for bearing this risk is his profit. "Profit," it has been said, "arises out of the inherent, absolute unpredictability of things."

3. Causes of dynamic change

The chief changes that cause uncertainty are:

(a) changes in population with the consequent changes in demand;

(b) improvements in the technique of production;

(c) changes in the demand of consumers as a result of changes of fashion, increasing incomes, etc.

If any of these changes can be foreseen pure profit will not arise; it is only unexpected changes that result in uncertainty and therefore bring about the opportunity for pure profit.

4. Profit and enterprise

In old-established industries pure profit tends to be very low or even to disappear. In such businesses conditions are fairly stable, and uncertainty, though still present, is at a minimum. There are big differences in the pure profit to be obtained in different industries as a result of differences in uncertainty. There are also wide differences in the pure profit earned by different entrepreneurs in the same industry due to differences in the efficiency of entrepreneurs. The possibility of pure profit carries with it the possibility of incurring loss. Pure profit can be considered the reward of enterprise. It is an inducement to entrepreneurs to establish new undertakings, where risk and uncertainty are high, but where pure profit also may be high. The possibility of greater profit also induces entrepreneurs to adopt new methods, and so improvement of technique is encouraged. Thus, profit is the driving force behind enterprise. Taxes on profit are therefore a check on enterprise.

5. Profit and costs of production

The first two elements of profit—wages of management and interest—are obviously costs of production. Pure profit is, however, a surplus that accrues only to the more successful entrepreneurs after all costs of production have been met, for the less successful will earn no pure profit. Success in producing this surplus is a matter of correct judgment. Therefore, pure profit cannot be reckoned a cost of production. The distinction becomes clearer if one considers the case of a business owned and controlled by one man. Suppose his capital to be £30,000 and that after paying all expenses of production there is a residue of £6,000. He will probably regard the whole of this as profit. If, then, the business is converted into a company, the previous sole proprietor becoming managing director, he may then be paid a salary of (say) £3,500, and if the turn-over of business is exactly the same as before the profit available for distribution will be £2,500. If interest on capital is calculated at 8%, then pure profit will be only £100.

6. Profit and rent

There is some similarity between pure profit and rent. Both are surpluses. Rent, however, is a surplus arising from the scarcity of a factor. Rent can accrue to any factor of production, whereas profit is the particular reward of the entrepreneur. Monopoly profit is more of a rent than a profit, since it is due to the scarcity of the product, although the scarcity is artificially created. Both rent and monopoly profit are unearned surpluses. Pure profit, however, is a surplus accruing only to the more successful entrepreneurs. Thus, pure profit is an earned surplus.

QUESTIONS

1. Distinguish between gross profit and net profit and show the connection, if any, between net profit and interest upon capital. (I.B.)

2. Distinguish between profit and interest and consider whether the *risk* factor is the same in the two cases. (I.B.)

3. Discuss the functions of the entrepreneur and the

method of his remuneration in the light of modern forms of business organisation. (C.I.S. Final.)

4. Explain the statement: "Profit is of the same genus as rent." (R.S.A. Adv.)

PART II

Banking, Finance and Trade

XIX. Origin and Functions of Money

1. Barter
In early days trade was carried on by barter, that is, goods were exchanged for goods. Barter was an awkward method of doing business since it meant that a carpenter making tables, and wishing to exchange a table for cloth, would find it necessary not only to approach a weaver of cloth but a weaver who also wished to acquire a table. Even after the carpenter had found such a man, there was a further difficulty: what was to be the rate of exchange between tables and cloth? An even greater problem occurs when a large article has to be exchanged for a very large quantity of a small commodity.

2. A Medium of exchange
The difficulties of barter led to the use of certain commodities to facilitate exchange. Anything that was generally acceptable and relatively scarce could serve this purpose, but in general goods that were easily marketable were most likely to serve as money. Thus money first came into use as a medium of exchange. Commodities selected as media of exchange were those that were valuable for their own sake. At different times and in different places, such things as cattle, salt, tea, sea-shells have all been used as money. Their disadvantages are obvious, and they were eventually superseded by the precious metals, silver and gold. These were less bulky, more durable, easily divisible, and their annual production from the mines was only a small proportion of the total quantity in existence.

3. Coinage
At first merchants paid for their purchases by a quantity of metal which they had to weigh out at each transaction, a pair of scales for the purpose being part of their normal

stock-in-trade. The next stage in the development of money was the cutting up of the metal into pieces of a fixed weight and fineness. So coins came into use. Coins in circulation, however, are subject to wear and tear; they are liable to be "clipped" by persons wishing to steal some of the valuable metal; and at various times monarchs have attempted to replenish their exchequers by deliberately debasing the coinage—that is, by lowering the amount of precious metal they were supposed to contain. Debasement of the coinage by the issuing authority always led to a fall in the value of such money, for merchants recognised the value of coins only for their metal and not at their face value. Where a coinage has been debased and new coins issued there is a tendency for the new coins to disappear from circulation. This is known as *Gresham's Law*, and is usually stated in the form: "bad money drives out good".

When the British sovereign and half-sovereign were in circulation they were worth their face value in gold, the replacement of worn coins being quite an expensive business. When, however, silver and bronze coins were minted they were only token coins, their value as metal being much less than their face value. At the present day only cheap metals are used for minting token coins. Consequently, such coins are only limited legal tender, cupro-nickel coins to a maximum of £5 (£10 for 50p coins) and bronze coins to a maximum of 20p.

4. Paper money
An important side of a goldsmith's business was the safe custody of money and valuables. Before the days of banks a client might deposit £100 (say) in gold for safe-keeping and receive in exchange a receipt for that amount. By endorsing the receipt he could assign his claim to the £100 to a third person. When it became customary to issue receipts in small denominations paper money had really come into existence, the goldsmith's receipt being the forerunner of the bank-note. The issue of bank-notes became an important and profitable part of the business of the early banks. At the present time the Bank of

England is the only bank in England with the right to issue bank-notes, though several Scottish banks still retain the privilege (*see* XXIV).

Bank-notes can be *convertible or inconvertible*. Before 1914 Bank of England notes were convertible, i.e. they could be exchanged on demand for an equivalent sum in gold. Since 1931 Bank of England notes have been inconvertible, and the promise printed on the notes is now almost meaningless. The Bank Charter Act of 1844 declared that all bank-notes had to have 100% gold backing, except for a small fiduciary issue. The fiduciary issue is that part of the note issue not backed by gold. During 1914–28 the British Government issued Treasury notes in denominations of £1 and ten shillings, but in 1928 this issue was taken over by the Bank of England, the fiduciary issue being increased by an equivalent amount. Since 1939 the fiduciary issue has increased enormously. In that year it stood at £260 million; by 1945 it had reached £1,400 million; by 1973 it was £4,000 million: and by 1978 it had increased to £7,675 million. Temporary increases are regularly made at Christmas and in the summer.

5. Bank deposits

At the present time approximately 90% of all payments in Great Britain are made by cheque. In this way bank deposits subject to transfer by cheque have come to be used as money. It should be noted that it is the bank deposit and not the cheque that serves as money. The cheque is simply a means by which money is transferred from one person's banking account to another's. The use of bank deposits as money is the latest stage in the development of money, and in countries such as Great Britain and the United States, bank deposits form the most important type of money in use today. When calculating the total volume of bank deposits it is usual to add together the total amounts on both current and deposit account.

6. Functions of money

There are four main functions of money:

(*a*) *A medium of exchange.* Money had its origin in the need for a medium of exchange. Money facilitates the exchange of goods, and thereby assists the development of trade.

(*b*) *A measure of value and a unit of account.* By assigning money prices to goods the second disadvantage of barter is overcome. The idea of money as a measure of value, however, is really fallacious, since value is subjective; but in practice money serves in a way as a measure of value. For purposes of calculation a unit of account is essential, and money best serves this purpose. For example, the only satisfactory way to calculate the value of the heterogeneous mass of goods and services that make up the national income is in terms of money. The unit of account, however, need not be the same as the currency, for if people lose faith in their currency as a result of a severe inflation, some other currency may come to be used as the unit of account. Even if there were no money, some sort of unit of account would still be necessary.

(*c*) *A store of value.* So long as one's assets are held in money one is free to exchange it for whatever other asset one pleases. For everyday needs, both individuals and business firms need to hold a certain amount of money, the amount depending on their liquidity-preference. However, history shows that in inflationary times money can turn out to be a very poor store of value.

(*d*) *A standard for deferred payments.* Money can perform this function only if its value in terms of goods is relatively stable. Only if this condition is fulfilled can future contracts in terms of money be made.

QUESTIONS

1. What are the functions of money? Write a short account of the English system of currency. (R.S.A. Inter.)

2. What do you consider to be the necessary characteristics of a good currency? (R.S.A. Inter.)

3. What do you understand by *money*? Would you include all or any of the following under the heading of money: (*a*) cheques; (*b*) postal orders; (*c*) bank-notes? Give reasons for your answers. (G.C.E. Ord.)

4. Explain the nature of money and describe its functions. (C.I.S. Final.)

5. "An exchange economy in which the division of labour is highly developed could not exist without money." Discuss. (G.C.E. Adv.)

6. What functions are performed by money? What things perform these functions in the United Kingdom? (G.C.E. Adv.)

XX. The value of money

1. The value of money and the price level

The values of different commodities are shown by their prices in terms of money. The value of money, therefore, can be seen only indirectly through the prices of other goods. If a certain quantity of goods at one period cost £5 and at a later period £7 this would show a decline in the value of money. The indicator of the value of money is thus the general price level, a general fall in prices showing an increase in the value of money, and a general rise in prices showing a decrease in its value. The value of money lies in the goods that can be obtained for it.

2. Changes in the value of money

Three distinct trends may be noticed in variations in the value of money:

(a) There has been a general tendency over the centuries for the value of money to fall. The level of prices in the sixteenth century was very low compared with the eighteenth, and prices in the eighteenth century were very low compared with those of the twentieth, though the long-term rise in prices has not been so regular as Fig. 8 seems to indicate.

(b) During the nineteenth and early twentieth centuries a medium-period movement was discernible, during

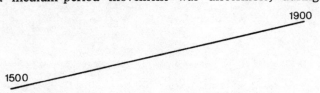

FIG. 8—*The Long-term Tendency of Prices to Rise.*

which for periods of twenty to twenty-five years prices were falling or rising (Fig. 9).

(*i*) *1820–49*. During this period prices were falling as a result of expanding production, the output of goods being more rapid than the output of gold on which the supply of money depended at that time.

(*ii*) *1849–74*. A period of rising prices, due to discoveries of gold in California and Australia, the development of limited liability, and the greater use of cheques. During this period the quantity of money increased more rapidly than the supply of goods.

(*iii*) *1874–96*. Another period of falling prices, due to an increased demand for gold, Germany adopting the Gold Standard in 1873 and France in 1878, together with an increased rate of production.

(*iv*) *1896–1914*. Prices were again rising, due to an increase in the quantity of money resulting from new discoveries of gold in South Africa.

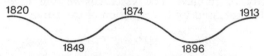

FIG. 9—*Medium-term Fluctuations in Prices.*

Before 1914 the quantity of money was closely associated with gold, and each of the two periods of rising prices coincided with an increased output of gold, in 1849 in Australia and California, in 1896 in South Africa.

(*c*) During the nineteenth century particularly, there was also a pronounced *short-period variation* of prices associated with the trade cycle, with a seven- to eight-year interval between depressions, and between booms.

During the upswing of the cycle business activity increases, employment rises, prices rise and the value of money falls. During the downswing business activity declines, unemployment increases, prices fall and the value of money rises.

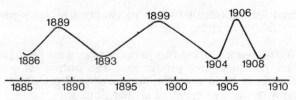

FIG. 10—*Short-term Variations in Prices.*

Since all three tendencies have to be superimposed upon one another, each depression tends to be at a higher level of prices than the previous one.

3. The quantity theory of money

In its crudest form this theory asserted that an increase in the quantity of money would produce a proportionate increase in prices. Irving Fisher modified the theory to include the influence of the velocity of circulation, an increase which has a similar effect to an increase in the quantity of money. The essentials of the theory are usually expressed by the equation of exchange:

$$MV = PT$$

where M is the amount of money (bank-notes, etc. + bank deposits); V is the velocity of circulation; T is the total number of trade transactions; P is the general price level. If T is unchanged, then P may rise as a result of either an increase in M or V. Again, if T remained unchanged, a decrease in M could be offset by an increase in V, and P would remain stable. Or again, an increase in M, with V unchanged, could be offset by an increase in T, and so leave P unchanged.

This equation probably explains the long-term changes in the value of money, but not the cyclical fluctuations.

By its monetary policy a country can increase or decrease the quantity of money, but not the velocity of circulation. Expectation of a future rise or fall of prices will affect the amount of money people desire to hold, and so the velocity of circulation, and through that prices. In a runaway inflation prices rise at a much faster rate than is warranted by the increase in the quantity of money, due to the general desire to hold as little money as possible owing to the expectation of a still further rise in prices.

4. Some criticisms of the quantity theory

A number of criticisms have been levelled against the quantity theory of money:

(*a*) It offers no explanation of the way in which the value of money is really determined, for it only explains changes in the value of money after a certain price level has been established.

(*b*) In its original form it is too rigid, i.e. it implies that an increase in the quantity of money produces a proportionate increase in prices. To double the quantity of money would not result in a doubling of all prices.

(*c*) It ignores the important psychological factor that expectation of future changes influences people's actions in the present.

(*d*) It takes no account of the effect of holding money.

(*e*) It approaches the problem from the side of supply and ignores the effects of demand.

(*f*) In its original form it takes no account of the influence of changes in the velocity of circulation.

The theory, however, contains one fundamental truth, viz. that there is some connection between the value of money and the supply of it; it does, therefore, explain the effect of the steep falls in the value of money that occur in inflationary conditions.

5. The money supply

The value of a commodity depends on the relative strengths of the forces of supply and demand. In the same way, perhaps, the value of money is determined by these two forces, though it must not be forgotten that money differs from other commodities in not being wanted for its own sake.

The money supply presents little difficulty. There are two main kinds of money in use in Great Britain at the present day: (i) cash—bank-notes and coin, and (ii) bank deposits transferable by cheque. Today bank deposits form more than four-fifths of the total supply of money. The supply of a commodity is related to its cost of production, whereas the supply of most money to-day depends on the policy of the monetary authorities—the State, and the central bank—and the banking system.

6. The demand for money

By demand for money is meant the demand to hold money as an alternative to investing it. The extent of people's preference for liquidity determines what proportion of their assets they will hold in the form of money. To hold money involves a loss of the interest it otherwise would have earned. Why, then, do people hold money? Lord Keynes gave three reasons for holding money:

(a) *The transactions motive.* A certain amount of money is needed for everyday requirements—bus fares, purchases of food, clothing, etc. Some of this money will be held in the form of cash and some in current accounts at banks.

(b) *The precautionary motive.* Most people prefer to keep rather more money than is required for ordinary purposes as a reserve against unforeseen contingencies.

(c) *The speculative motive.* The amount of money people hold for reasons (a) and (b) is fairly stable in the short period, so that the main influence on the amount of money held is the speculative motive. The amount held for this reason depends on people's expectations of changes in the rate of interest. If they expect the prices of stocks and shares to fall in the future (i.e. a rise in the rate of yield) they will tend to hold more money; if they expect the prices of stocks and shares to rise (i.e. a fall in the rate of yield) they will tend to hold less money.

7. Effects of changes on the value of money

Changes in the value of money affect both production and distribution:

(a) *Effects on production.* Rising prices stimulate production, whereas falling prices check production and increase unemployment. The reason for this is that costs do not change so rapidly or in the same proportion as commodity prices, so that when prices are rising profits tend to be higher, and when prices are falling tend to be lower than was anticipated.

(b) *Effects on distribution.* Changes in the value of money affect different groups of people differently:

(i) Those with fixed incomes in terms of money find that the value of their incomes increases when prices are falling, but if prices are rising the value of their incomes declines. There are, however, fewer people today on rigidly fixed incomes than formerly.

(ii) Those whose incomes depend on profits find that their real incomes increase when prices are rising, for profits increase more rapidly than prices.

(iii) Wage-earners in the past have often found that there was a time-lag between a rise in prices and a rise in wages, but in a period of prolonged inflation wages may increase more rapidly than prices.

8. Types of inflation

The term inflation has three meanings:

(a) Monetary expansion associated with, and controlled by, an inflow of gold to a country on the gold standard (controlled inflation of a limited extent).

(b) A condition where the volume of purchasing power is constantly running ahead of the output of goods and services (persistent inflation).

(c) Hyperinflation (or runaway inflation) where money eventually becomes worthless. Germany, Hungary, Greece and some other countries have suffered this kind of inflation.

The inflationary spiral. Pressure of demand resulting from an excessive expansion of the money supply forces up the prices of goods and services. High prices then lead to demands for higher wages, which increase costs of production and so force prices up again.

These conditions are most likely to occur in times of war or during a post-war period when Government expenditure is too great to be covered from taxation.

9. Inflation in Great Britain

A number of causes have contributed to the persistence of inflation in Great Britain since 1945:

(*a*) *A world condition.* Since 1945, inflation has been the outstanding monetary feature of the world, though the degree of inflation has varied greatly between one country and another. In such conditions it is extremely difficult for a single country to keep inflation under control within its own borders, especially in the case of a large importing country such as Great Britain where higher prices of imported raw materials and higher prices of imported foodstuffs increase costs of production and hence raise the cost of living.

(*b*) *Increase in the money supply.* Over the past thirty years Great Britain has experienced a huge increase in the money supply. Some writers regard this as the primary cause of inflation. It is significant that during 1974–77, one of the worst periods of inflation, there was a huge increase in the money supply. In its anxiety to maintain full employment after 1945, and in the 1970s to reduce unemployment, the Government tended to adopt an expansionary monetary policy even though it was well aware that it would be a stimulus to inflation. During the same period the national debt showed its largest ever increase in peacetime, the result in the 1970s of huge budget deficits with heavy borrowing in consequence.

(*c*) *Government responsibility for full employment.* This is an important cause of persistent inflation. In such conditions demands for higher wages are more likely to be met, especially when these can be passed on in the form of higher prices. The result is that the wages–prices spiral is stimulated. The Government will deal with any temporary falling away from full employment by stimulating demand, thereby also stimulating a further round of inflation.

(d) *Trade unions.* The situation has been aggravated by the growing power of the trade unions, resulting in continual demands for wage increases which, rather surprisingly, the high level of unemployment in the 1970s did not check. Attempts to control inflation by means of pay pauses or an incomes policy or more recently the "social contract" between the Government and the trade unions have met with only temporary success, generally being followed by further severe bouts of inflation. If increases in incomes exceed the rate of growth of the real national income, inflation is inevitable.

10. Measurement of changes in the value of money

Attempts have been made to measure changes in the value of money by compiling index numbers. A group of commodities is taken and the number 100 is assigned to the base year selected. The best known index number is probably that compiled by the Department of Employment to show changes in the level of retail prices. It takes account of the prices of food, clothing, rent, fuel, light and a number of miscellaneous items. The base taken for the original "cost of living" index was July 1914. The index has been modified on a number of occasions. The main changes were (i) slightly lower weights for food and tobacco; (ii) rather heavier weights for fuel, light, transport; and (iii) inclusion of a few new commodities.

The chief difficulties associated with the compilation of index numbers are:

(a) The choice of commodities to be included.

(b) The difficulty of "weighting"—i.e. the amounts of the various commodities to take into account. Table IX shows the different "weights" adopted for the index at various dates. The weights of the various items in the index are now revised annually.

TABLE IX. *Cost of Living Index.*

Commodity groups	1914	1952	1956	1962	1971	1976
	%	%	%	%	%	%
I. Food	60	39.9	35.0	31.9	25.0	22.8
II. Alcoholic drink	—	}16.8	7.1	6.4	6.5	8.0
III. Tobacco			8.0	7.9	5.9	4.6
IV. Housing	16	7.2	8.7	10.2	11.9	11.2
V. Fuel and light	8	6.6	5.5	6.2	6.0	5.6
VI. Durable household goods	—	6.2	6.6	6.4	6.1	7.6
VII. Clothing and footwear	12	9.8	10.6	9.8	8.7	8.4
VIII. Transport and vehicles	—	—	6.8	9.2	13.6	14.0
IX. Miscellaneous	4	4.4	5.9	6.4	6.5	7.4
X. Services	—	9.1	5.8	5.6	5.4	5.7
XI. Meals outside home	—	—	—	—	4.4	4.7
	100	100	100	100	100	100

(*c*) The difficulty of accurately comparing one period with another for the following reasons—

(*i*) New commodities come on to the market.

(*ii*) Changes in taste or fashion influence the demand for some commodities.

(*iii*) Changes in the composition of the various income groups in the community affect the demand for many commodities.

(*iv*) People buy different assortments of goods. As a result, price changes have different effects for different people. This makes it difficult to compare the cost of living in different countries.

(*v*) A change in quality is equivalent to a change in price, but this would not be reflected in the index number.

The original cost-of-living index of 1914 was a better reflection of the cost of living of a working-class family than of a family of moderate means. The percentage of income spent on food, for example, declines as income increases.

On account of their many drawbacks, index numbers are of little use for comparisons over long periods of time. However, they serve as a rough guide for comparing points of time that are close together, for example, month-to-month fluctuations.

QUESTIONS

1. Discuss the meaning and consequences of the inflation of a currency. (R.S.A. Adv.)

2. Investigate the effects of large-scale inflation upon the production of wealth and the distribution of income.

3. What is the Quantity Theory? Do you think that the Theory gives an adequate explanation of the forces determining the value of money? (C.I.S. Final.)

4. How would you define "value of money"? How is it measured? Give illustrations. (C.I.S. Inter.)

5. What are the principal causes that may bring about a change in the value of money? By what means are these changes measured?

XXI. Banking

1. Early development of banking in England

In the Middle Ages British trade was mainly financed by foreign bankers. When banking developed in London it originated with the goldsmiths, who carried out many of the functions of modern banks—accepting deposits, issuing receipts which later came to be used as bank-notes, and making loans.

In other parts of England banks developed from the businesses of merchants and manufacturers; for example, Samuel Lloyd, a Birmingham ironmaster, established a bank from which Lloyds Bank originated. Provincial banking grew rapidly during and after the Industrial Revolution in the late eighteenth and early nineteenth centuries, when many London private banks opened country branches.

The first joint-stock bank to be founded in England was the Bank of England, which dates from 1694, and for 136 years it had no branch outside London. In the meantime many private banks were established, but those set up in London were forbidden to issue notes. Most of these early banks were very small, and in times of crisis large numbers of them failed.

2. Joint-stock banking

An Act of 1708 declared that no corporate institution or partnership of more than six partners was to undertake banking business in England, with the result that the Bank of England obtained an almost complete monopoly except for a number of small local institutions. In Scotland, however, the Bank of Scotland, founded in 1695, had no monopoly of joint-stock banking, which developed there at an earlier date than in England. A campaign in favour of joint-stock banking in England

resulted in the Act of 1826. This permitted the establishment of joint-stock banks with unlimited liability, provided that they were situated beyond 65 miles from
London. These banks were granted the right to issue
notes, and the act also permitted the Bank of England
to open branches, thirteen being opened between 1826
and 1843. After 1826 many joint-stock banks were established. In 1833 joint-stock banks were allowed to open
in London, provided that they did not issue notes. In
1856 the right to limited liability was granted to any company carrying on a trading business, and in 1858 the privilege was extended to joint-stock banks.

Small banks, whether private or joint-stock, were
unable to withstand crises, and many failures occurred.
Larger banks began to appear as a result of the amalgamation of small banks, and many private banks became
joint-stock banks, as, for example, Lloyds and Barclays.
Many joint-stock banks amalgamated with private banks
which were members of the London Bankers' Clearing
House with the result that by the end of the nineteenth
century a small number of large banks with headquarters
in London had come into being. After the First World
War another period of amalgamation set in, culminating
in 1921 in the creation of the "Big Five"—Midland,
Barclays, Lloyds, National Provincial and Westminster,
reduced in 1968 to the "Big Four" by the amalgamation
of the National Provincial and the Westminster to form
the National Westminster. Of the other English commercial banks the largest is Williams & Glyn's. There are also
a number of regional savings banks.

3. Types of bank
There are several different types of bank:

(a) *Savings banks*, which accept deposits, and, until
recently, did little other banking business, e.g. National
Savings Bank, Trustee Savings Banks.

(b) *Commercial banks.* Granting credit is the chief
function of the large joint-stock or commercial banks, but
they undertake all kinds of banking business.

(*c*) *Merchant banks*, or Accepting Houses which specialise in business connected with bills of exchange. Nowadays they also do a considerable amount of ordinary banking business.

(*d*) *Secondary banks*, some of which were formerly hire-purchase finance houses, and which accept deposits.

(*e*) *Central banks*, which are responsible for a country's monetary policy, and exercise control over the commercial banks, e.g. the Bank of England, the Bank of France, etc.

4. Functions of banks: (i) Accepting deposits

Accepting deposits is the oldest function of banks. Two types of account are available:

(*a*) *Deposit or savings accounts.* Usually notice of withdrawal is required and interest is paid on them, the amount varying with the prevailing rate of interest.

(*b*) *Current accounts*, from which withdrawals by cheque can be made. Interest is not usually paid on these accounts and the banks generally make a charge to customers for clearing cheques unless a fairly large credit balance is maintained.

In calculating the volume of deposits of the banks it is usual to add together the two types of deposits, since in practice sums can easily be transferred from one type of account to the other.

5. Functions of banks: (ii) The issue of notes

This was an important function of most early banks, but in England the only bank now retaining the right to issue notes is the Bank of England.

A bank-note is really a type of promissory note (exempt from Stamp Duty), i.e. it is a debt that the bank owes to the bearer of the note. In most countries there are legal restrictions on the issue of bank-notes (*see* XXIV).

6. Functions of banks: (iii) Advances to customers

Banks carry out this function in the following ways:

(a) *By loan.* This being for a fixed sum, interest has to be paid on the whole amount borrowed. In addition to loans to businessmen, most banks also grant personal loans.

(b) *By overdraft.* This permits the borrower to draw cheques for an agreed amount in excess of the sum standing to his credit in his current account. Interest is paid only on the actual amount overdrawn.

(c) *By discounting bills of exchange.* The use of a bill of exchange enables the debtor to postpone payment for a period, and yet, if a bank is willing to discount the bill, the creditor can receive immediate payment, less the discount charged by the bank.

(d) *By financing hire-purchase transactions.* Since 1958 the leading English banks have had subsidiary hire-purchase finance companies. Hire-purchase business has increased enormously during the past twenty-five years.

7. Functions of banks: (iv) Agents for customers

Banks also provide a number of other services for their customers, some of the chief being:

(a) the purchase or sale of stock-exchange securities;
(b) the issue of travellers' cheques, bank drafts, etc;
(c) foreign-exchange business;
(d) acting as trustees or executors;
(e) acting as reference to a firm seeking to obtain credit from another firm.

8. Loans make deposits

Bank deposits are created in the following ways:

(a) When a customer makes a payment in cash into his deposit or current account.

(b) When a customer pays a cheque that he has received into his banking account. The account of the drawer of the cheque is depleted by an equivalent amount, but if an overdraft has been granted the customer will be able to draw cheques for this additional amount, and when these are deposited by the payees total deposits will be increased. In this way *"loans make deposits"*, and so the banks are themselves mainly responsible for the creation of bank deposits.

(*c*) When a bank purchases securities it pays for them by a cheque drawn on itself; the payee's account will be increased by this amount, and total deposits will again be increased.

Bank deposits are of enormous economic significance, since they can be used as purchasing power. They form the principal form of money in many countries today.

9. Bank credit

There are two kinds of credit:

(*a*) *Trade credit*. In this case the seller forgoes payment for a time in favour of the buyer. When a wholesaler grants credit to a retailer the wholesaler forgoes the use of the money owed him by the retailer until payment is made. Trade credit therefore results in no increase in the volume of purchasing power.

(*b*) *Bank credit*. If banks restricted their loans to the amount of their cash deposits, bank credit would be similar to trade credit, the use of the money merely being transferred from one person to another. Since, however, banks are prepared to grant loans up to twelve and a half times their cash reserve, clearly they create credit and so increase the quantity of money.

10. Restrictions on the creation of credit by banks

The power of banks to create credit is restricted in a number of ways:

(*a*) *The banks' liquidity rules*. It has been seen that bank loans increase deposits, with the result that bank deposits greatly exceed the total amount of cash in existence. Banking is conducted on the assumption that only a small proportion of depositors will demand cash at any given time. So long as a bank possesses the confidence of its depositors this will be so, for no bank, however soundly managed, is capable of withstanding a "run" on it.

To maintain this confidence a bank must always be prepared to pay cash on demand. It is for this purpose a cash reserve is held, and it is customary for British banks to maintain a definite ratio between their reserves and their deposits. This is known as the cash ratio. The 8% cash ratio is the first liquidity rule of the banks. For a long time they also maintained a second liquidity rule of 28% between their more liquid assets—cash, money at call, and bills discounted—and their deposits. In 1971, however, the Bank of England introduced a new liquidity rule: the commercial banks were to maintain a ratio of $12\frac{1}{2}\%$ between their deposits and their more liquid assets together with Government stocks within one year of maturity and some eligible commercial bills.

(b) *The Clearing House.* The banks must expand or contract credit together. If, for example, one of the "Big Four" banks expands credit more than the other three its additional loans will create additional deposits to the value of this excess. On average, only one-fifth of the cheques drawn on these new deposits will be paid back into accounts of its own customers. The remaining four-fifths will be paid into other banks, and this will result in an adverse balance at the Clearing House and a depletion of its cash reserves at the Bank of England. A bank's reserve at the Bank of England forms about half its cash reserve, and this reduction in its reserve would compel the bank to reduce its loans in order to maintain its customary liquidity ratio. On the other hand, if a bank is unduly cautious and lags behind the others in creating credit its cash reserve will grow at the expense of its profit-earning assets, and its profits will compare unfavourably with those of other banks. The banks must therefore keep in step.

(c) *Collateral security.* Before a bank grants a loan it usually requires the borrower to offer some kind of collateral security, which the bank can convert into cash in case of default. This may take the form of stock-exchange securities, insurance policies, deeds of property, etc. Unless the banks are willing to lower their security standards, the extent of their loans will be limited by the amount of collateral security available to borrowers.

(d) *The monetary authorities.* The final and principal restriction comes from the monetary authorities—the Bank of England and the Treasury (*see* XXIV, 11).

QUESTIONS

1. "A bank can create money, but only within limits." Examine this quotation with special reference to the English banking system. (I.B.)

2. Explain "bank clearing". (G.C.E. Adv.)

3. To what extent, if any, can the banks create credit? (C.I.S. Final.)

4. Discuss the view that the commercial banks can only lend the money which others have loaned to them. (G.C.E. Adv.)

XXII. The English Banking System:
(i) The Commercial Banks

The English banking system comprises three groups of institutions: (i) the commercial or joint-stock banks; (ii) the London money market; and (iii) the central bank, the Bank of England.

1. The theory of banking
The aim of a commercial bank is to earn profits for its shareholders. The most profitable of its assets is advances to customers, but this is its least liquid asset, and a bank must always be prepared to pay cash on demand. Liquidity of assets is the banker's guiding principle. The desire to increase profits is an incentive to a bank to expand its most profitable asset, but this is checked by its desire for liquidity. Thus, a bank maintains a large proportion of its assets in short-term loans and bills in addition to its cash reserve. Long-term loans and investments are thus not widely favoured by banks.

2. The balance sheet of a bank
The items in the balance sheet of a commercial bank are of great economic importance.

(a) *Liabilities.* The capital, reserve and deposits comprise the chief items of a bank's liabilities, but deposits form over 95% of the total. Some deposits are held on current account and some on deposit account. During the past 25 years there has been a huge increase in the total deposits of the English commercial banks. By 1977 total deposits of the London Clearing Banks exceeded £25,000 million.

(b) *Assets.* The principal assets of a bank, in order of liquidity, comprise cash in hand and at the Bank of

England, money at call and short notice, bills discounted, investments, and advances to customers. In 1960 a new asset appeared in the balance sheet—Special Deposits at the Bank of England. Table X shows the distribution at various dates of the combined assets of the London Clearing Banks.

TABLE X. *The Combined Assets of the London Clearing Banks.*

	£ million		
	1951	*1973*	*1977*
Coin, notes, and balances with Bank of England	488	868	2,019
Money at call and short notice	276	1,009	1,011
Bills discounted	501	803	925
Special Deposits	—	135	608
Investments	680	1,290	2,545
Advances to customers	1,920	9,636	16,775
Other assets	316	1,150	1,357

3. A bank's assets
The following are the main assets of a commercial bank:

(*a*) *Coin, notes, etc.* Cash is a bank's most liquid asset, and about half of it consists of cash in hand, distributed among the various branches of the banks, the remainder being its reserve at the Bank of England. This asset yields no profit to a bank, and so it will be kept as small a proportion of its total assets as is consistent with safety. Hence the maintenance of a cash ratio.

(*b*) *Money at call and short notice.* This asset consists chiefly of short-term loans to discount houses and bill brokers, that is, to the London money market. This is the bank's second most liquid asset, forming a useful second line of defence. Such loans can easily be called in without loss, and where, as in England, there is a well-developed money market it enables the banks to keep a smaller proportion of their total assets in the form of cash. Because of its liquidity this asset earns only a small profit.

(c) *Bills discounted.* These are a very desirable asset to a banker, yielding a profit and yet being fairly liquid. They have, too, the advantage of having a fixed date when they fall due, and so they are said to be self-liquidating. Bankers prefer bills to ordinary loans because they have their origin in actual trade transactions, and if necessary they can be re-discounted. The banks receive most of their bills from the discount houses. Most bills nowadays are Treasury bills.

These three assets—cash, call money, bills discounted—are the more liquid assets of a bank and generally form about 28% of the total.

(d) *Special deposits.* Since 1960 the Bank of England has had the power to demand special deposits from the English and Scottish commercial banks. Unlike balances at the Bank of England, these special deposits cannot be regarded as cash, since they cannot be drawn upon until released by the Bank of England.

(e) *Investments.* Bank investments are mainly in British Government securities, usually those with not more than five years to run to maturity, since banks generally do not care for long-term investments.

(f) *Advances to customers.* In Great Britain bank loans are generally restricted to the provision of working capital. It is not usual for British banks to provide fixed capital. Banks lend to farmers, all branches of industry, wholesalers, retailers and to professional and personal borrowers. Both directly and indirectly through their subsidiaries, banks help to finance hire-purchase transactions.

Investments and advances comprise the less liquid but more profitable assets of a bank. They tend to vary inversely with one another. When advances are in great demand banks usually reduce their investments; when fewer desirable borrowers are to be found they increase their investments.

4. Branch banking

Commercial banking in England is now carried on by a small number of banks, each with a country-wide network of branches. In the United States, though there has been some development of branch banking in recent years, most of the banks are of the single-unit type. The main advantages of branch banking are:

(*a*) Lower cash reserves are required at each branch, since one branch can assist another in case of need.

(*b*) Risk of failure is reduced. Where industry is localised, banks in one district may suffer heavy losses if the basic industry declines. In the case of unit banks this may mean a crop of failures, such as occurred in the United States between the two wars, whereas a bank with widespread branches may be able to offset losses in a depressed area by profits in a more prosperous one.

In favour of unit banks it can be said, too, that they can develop greater knowledge of local conditions, and so provide better services for local industry, but the advantages of branch banking easily outweigh the advantages of the unit bank.

QUESTIONS

1. What are the ways in which British banks hold their assets? How have the proportions of their assets held in different ways varied in recent years, and why?

2. How do banks assist business firms? (G.C.E. Ord.)

3. Comment on the statement that the functions of the joint-stock banks are reflected in their balance sheets. (G.C.E. Adv.)

XXIII. The English Banking System:
(ii) The London Money Market

1. What is a money market?

A money market is essentially a market for very short-term loans. The chief commodity dealt in is the bill of exchange—trade bills and Treasury bills. Business is principally in the hands of bill brokers, discount and accepting houses and the commercial banks, with the Bank of England as lender of last resort.

2. Members of the London money market

(a) *Discount houses, bill brokers and running brokers.* The discount houses and bill brokers discount bills, borrowing the money "at call or short notice" for the purpose from the commercial banks. Running brokers are simply agents acting on behalf of others.

(b) *Accepting houses.* These are generally known as merchant bankers. For the payment of a small commission to an accepting house a bill of exchange can be "accepted" by one of these institutions, and the bill then becomes more negotiable. The leading accepting houses have their own agents in the chief commercial centres abroad, and in this way obtain information regarding the credit-worthiness of merchants in all parts of the world. A foreign merchant can open an acceptance credit with an accepting house, upon which an English merchant can then draw a bill. Where a foreign bank, the credit of which is better known than that of a foreign merchant, deals with an accepting house a re-imbursement credit is obtained.

(c) *Commercial banks.* In addition to engaging in acceptance business on their own account, the main service provided by the commercial banks to the money market is making short-term loans (known in their balance sheets as "money at call and short notice") to the other members of the market.

(*d*) *Bank of England*. When the commercial banks call in their loans to the money market the discount houses are compelled to borrow from the Bank of England, the lender of last resort.

3. Types of bills: (i) The promissory note

These are more popular in the United States than in Great Britain. A promissory note usually takes the form shown in Fig. 11.

£264

Green Road,
Leeds, 2.

8 April, 19....

Three months after date I promise to pay Martin Chuzzle-

wit or order Two Hundred and Sixty-Four Pounds, value

received.

Mark Tapley.

Payable at West Riding Bank, Ltd., Leeds.

FIG. 11—*A Promissory Note.*

A promissory note falls due three days ("days of grace") after the expiry of the period stated. It is a negotiable instrument, and it can be discounted at any time.

4. Types of bills: (ii) The bill of exchange

The bill of exchange, like a promissory note, is a negotiable instrument, is drawn for a specified period, entitles the debtor to three days' grace and can be discounted. It differs from the promissory note by being drawn by the creditor and requires to be accepted by the debtor (*see* Fig. 12). Bills accepted by a bank or recognised accepting house are first-class or bank bills, and most bills coming on to the London Money Market are of this type.

5. Types of bills: (iii) Treasury bills

These are issued by the Treasury for sums of £5,000 or

£10,000, £25,000, £50,000 and £100,000, for periods of three months. A certain amount is offered each week, tenders being invited, and the bills issued to the highest bidders, who can have the bills dated for any day the

£380

Three months after

order Three Hundred

value received.

To N. Winkle, Esq.,
    Cross Lane,
        Huddersfield.

*Accepted payable at West Riding Bank Ltd., Huddersfield.
N. Winkle.*

34 City Road,
Manchester, 3.
7 June, 19....

date, pay to me or my

and Eighty Pounds,

T. Tupman.

FIG. 12—*A Bill of Exchange.*

following week. Treasury bills were created by the Treasury Bill Act of 1877. The Government's revenue comes in irregularly, and expenditure in anticipation of revenue is financed by Treasury bills. Over the years, however, Treasury bills have been increasingly used by the Government as a means of short-term borrowing, and now greatly exceed trade bills on the London Money Market.

6. The money market in the British banking system

The intervention of the money market between the commercial banks and the central bank is a distinctive feature of the English banking system. To increase their cash reserves English banks call in their loans to the money market, whereas in countries lacking a well-developed money market the commercial banks borrow direct from the central bank.

The amount of business transacted on the London Money Market is much greater than that carried on in foreign financial centres. The existence of a well-developed money market enables English banks to maintain a lower cash reserve than most foreign banks.

7. The business of the money market

Bill brokers are able to make a profit by charging a slightly higher rate of discounting bills than that at which they borrow from the banks. The banks themselves discount bills, but do not care to have bills with more than two months to run; they also prefer to have bills in "parcels" with about equal amounts falling due each week. In effect they pay bill brokers a fee for collecting bills, holding them for the first month and arranging them in "parcels" to meet the needs of the banks. It is unusual for a bank to dispose of a bill once it has acquired it.

8. Recent developments in the London money market

During the past fifty years there has been a very serious decline in the use of the bill of exchange as a means of payment both for inland and foreign transactions. The cheque has replaced the inland bill, and the bank draft and telegraphic transfer have largely superseded the foreign bill. To offset this there has been a huge increase in the issue of Treasury bills.

The decline in foreign trade bills has weakened the position of the accepting houses, for Treasury bills do not require to be accepted. Unlike trade bills, Treasury bills are issued for convenient amounts and dated to suit those discounting them. Thus the services of the discount houses are less necessary to the banks than formerly.

The decline of their specialist business in the money market led accepting houses to develop other activities such as dealing in short-dated Government stocks and expanding their ordinary banking business. They assist firms wishing to merge and they often act as advisers and trustees of pension funds. Further business has accrued to the merchant banks from the development of new negotiable instruments such as certificates of deposit and bills drawn on local authorities, and in the international field, the emergence of Euro-currency deposits, especially Euro-dollars. These are funds denominated in the currencies of the countries of origin but which have been deposited in other countries; they are negotiable and are of particular advantage to multinational companies.

The continued existence of the money market is largely dependent, therefore, on the goodwill of the banks, which do not tender directly for Treasury bills but allow the discount houses to do so. The discount houses hold these bills for one month and then rediscount them with the banks. It is doubtful, however, whether the money market could have survived had it not developed new lines of business.

The money market provides the banks with a very liquid asset—money at call and short notice. It also results in British banks never having to borrow from the Bank of England.

QUESTIONS

1. What institutions are found in the London Money Market? State briefly their functions and their relations. (R.S.A. Adv.)

2. What do you mean by the money market? Describe the precise functions performed by the institutions that are usually regarded as comprising the money market. (I.B.)

XXIV. The English Banking System: (iii) The Bank of England

1. Functions of a central bank

Most countries now have central banks, generally State-owned as, for example, the Bank of England (since 1946), the Bank of France and the U.S. Federal Reserve System. A central bank must work closely with the Government, for its main function is to assist in carrying out the monetary policy of the country. A central bank must have some means of controlling the commercial banks; it must be subject to State control, whether nationalised or not. The nationalisation of the Bank of England brought about no serious change in its relations with the Government. A central bank should not compete with the commercial banks for ordinary banking business, nor should it strive to maximise its profits.

2. The Bank Charter Act 1844

A large number of banks, each with the right to issue bank-notes, it was felt, made for monetary instability. To control the note issue, the Bank Charter Act 1844 was passed. Its chief provisions were:

(a) It divided the work of the Bank of England into two departments: (i) Issue Department, and (ii) Banking Department.

(b) There was to be a small fiduciary issue (about £14 million), but all notes above this amount were to be backed by gold.

(c) No new bank was to be allowed to issue notes; existing issues were not to be increased; a bank outside London amalgamating with one with a London office was to lose its right to issue notes.

(d) The Bank of England was to be allowed to increase

its fiduciary issue by two-thirds of the amount of the lapsed issue of any bank ceasing to issue notes. In 1844 there were seventy-two banks of issue in England, but by 1914 the number had been reduced to thirteen. By 1921 the Bank of England had become the sole bank of issue in England, although Scottish banks still possessed limited powers to issue notes.

(e) The Bank of England had to publish a weekly return for both its issue and banking departments.

3. The Currency and Bank-Notes Act 1928

This act enabled the Bank of England to take over this Treasury issue. During the period 1914–28, the Treasury issued notes in denominations of £1 and 10s. (50p) to replace the gold coinage. The chief provisions of the Act were:

(a) the fiduciary issue was to be increased to £260 million; backed by securities or silver to a maximum value of £5½ million;

(b) all notes in excess of this amount were to be fully backed by gold;

(c) the fiduciary issue could be varied only with the consent of the Treasury.

4. The work of the Bank of England

The following are the principal functions of the Bank of England:

(a) It is the Government's bank, that is, the Government keeps an account at the Bank of England.

(b) It is the only bank in England with the right to issue bank-notes.

(c) It is the bankers' bank. The English commercial banks keep balances at the Bank of England.

(d) It holds the country's reserves.

(e) It acts as "lender of last resort" to the money market.

(f) It assists the Government in carrying out the country's monetary policy.

Nowadays it undertakes only a small amount of ordinary banking business, and it rarely accepts new customers.

5. The weekly bank return

The Bank Charter Act 1844, required the Bank of England to publish separate weekly balance sheets for its two departments. This is the Bank Return which is published every Wednesday. Consider the weekly return for the Issue Department:

I. ISSUE DEPARTMENT
Wednesday, 17 August 19–7

	£ m		£ m
Notes issued:			
In circulation	7,314	(b) Government debt	11
(a) In Banking Department	11	(c) Government securities	6,271
		(d) Other securities	1,043
	7,325		7,325

(a) This is the unused portion of the note issue.

(b) These are loans made to the Government by the Bank during its first 150 years of existence.

(c) These are Government bonds.

(d) Mostly issued by Commonwealth Governments.

(b), (c) and (d) These items together form the fiduciary issue. Since 1971 the note issue has been entirely fiduciary.

(e) Most of the bank's gold was transferred in 1939 to the Treasury's Exchange Equalisation Account. Since 1971 the Issue Department has held no gold at all.

Consider now the return for the Banking Department:

II. BANKING DEPARTMENT
Wednesday, 17 August 19–7

		£ m			£ m
(a)	Capital	14½	(f)	Government securities	1,579
(b)	Rest	3½	(g)	Other securities	151
(c)	Public deposits	16	(h)	Discounts and advances	231
(da)	Bankers' deposits	287	(i)	Notes	11
(db)	Special deposits	1,092	(j)	Gold and silver coin	1
(e)	Other accounts	560			
		1,973			1,973

(*a*) This is the amount originally subscribed by the stockholders. On the nationalisation of the Bank it was exchanged for Government stock.

(*b*) The Bank's reserve.

(*c*) This is the Government's balance. It increases as taxes come in, and decreases whenever the Government makes a payment or when interest is paid on Government stocks. Thus, it is the Government's bank.

(*da*) This item comprises the balances of the commercial banks. It is, therefore, the banker's bank.

(*db*) These are compulsory deposits made by the commercial banks and are known as special deposits.

(*e*) These are the balances of ordinary customers of the Bank.

(*f*) These comprise Government stocks and Treasury bills acquired directly as a result of ways and means advances to the Government.

(*g*) Securities acquired by the bank by "open market operations" (*see* p.146)

(*h*) Bills discounted and advances. This item indicates the extent to which the Bank is acting as "lender of last resort" (*see* p.144).

(*i*) This is the unused portion of the note issue.

(*j*) This now consists almost entirely of cupro-nickel and bronze coins available for issue to the commercial banks as required.

6. The Government's bank

The Bank of England was founded in 1694 for the purpose of lending money to the Government. Today it acts as the Government's banker, receiving the proceeds of taxation, managing the Government's account (Public Deposits) and the National Debt. The Government draws on its account to meet its expenditure. The Bank of England also floats loans for the Government, and sometimes lends, but only to a limited extent, by ways and means advances.

7. The note issue

After 1844 the note issue was partly backed by gold and partly fiduciary, that is, backed by securities. Down to

1914 the fiduciary issue was small; between 1928 and 1939 it formed rather less than half the total; but at the present day the entire note issue is fiduciary. Variations in the fiduciary issue require the assent of the Treasury. It has become customary to make temporary increases in the fiduciary issue at Christmas and in the summer to meet the increased demand for cash at these times.

8. The bankers' bank
The Bank of England, as the bankers' bank, offers the commercial banks banking facilities similar to those they themselves provide for their own customers.

The commercial banks keep part of their cash reserves at the Bank of England, and as a result settlements between the banks at the Clearing House can easily be made by adjusting their reserves. The huge volume of payments made by cheque can thus be effected without any actual movement of currency from one place to another. At the Clearing House the banks offset cheques drawn against one another, and settle only the difference by a cheque drawn on the Bank of England, the amount being deducted from the reserve of one bank and added to that of another. When a bank finds itself short of cash it makes a withdrawal in cash from its balance at the Bank of England.

9. The gold reserve
The country's gold and currency reserves are held at the Bank of England. Before 1932 the gold was the property of the Bank itself. Between 1932 and 1939 it was partly owned by the Bank and partly by the Treasury's Exchange Equalisation Account. From 1939 to 1971 the Bank of England itself possessed very little gold, and since 1971 it has been entirely owned by the Treasury.

10. Lender of last resort
If, in order to replenish their cash the commercial banks call in some of their loans to the Money Market, the discount houses will have to borrow from the Bank of England, the market then being said to be "in the Bank".

The Bank of England acts as *lender of last resort* only to the discount houses. In performing this function the Bank of England will discount (or more correctly, re-discount) first-class or bank bills for the discount houses at its minimum lending rate, formerly known as bank rate. Acting as lender of last resort is a vital function of a central bank, but it can, of course, impose its own terms.

11. Monetary policy

One of the most important functions of a central bank is its responsibility for monetary policy. Before 1914 the Bank of England was solely responsible for monetary policy; between 1919 and 1939 the Bank of England acted after consultation with the Treasury; since 1944, when the Government became responsible for the maintenance of full employment, monetary policy has been the joint responsibility of the British monetary authorities—the Chancellor of the Exchequer, the Treasury and the Bank of England.

Aims of monetary policy. Monetary policy primarily means deciding whether to increase or decrease the volume of purchasing power in the country. The aim might be:

(*a*) To protect the country's reserves and attract foreign funds to London.

(*b*) To stimulate production and so help to maintain full employment.

(*c*) To keep inflation in check.

Since 1945 all these aims have at different times been pursued, though in the 1970s they were often in conflict.

12. Instruments of monetary policy

The traditional instruments of monetary policy employed by the Bank of England were changes in interest rates and open-market operations.

(*a*) *Changes in interest rates.* The minimum rate at which the Bank of England will rediscount first-class bills for the discount houses was formerly known as bank rate. Its main importance used to be the fact that other rates of interest rose or fell with it. Bank rate changes used to be announced each Thursday. When the rate was high money was said to be dear, and when it was low, cheap. A high rate checks borrowing from the commercial banks, thereby reducing the volume of bank deposits. A low rate stimulates borrowing and so led to an increase in the volume of bank deposits. Many economists doubted the efficacy of bank rate as an instrument of monetary policy, and between 1932 and 1951 it ceased to be used for this purpose, being held at 2% for most of that time. Its use was revived in 1951.

In 1972, however, the banks ceased to relate their rates of interest to bank rate, adopting instead their own *base rate*. Bank rate then became solely the Bank of England's minimum lending rate as "lender of last resort". Instead of being arbitrarily determined it was in future to be the average rate of discount for Treasury bills. The authorities, however, retained the right to revert to the old system if this course should be considered necessary.

(*b*) *Open-market operations.* The aim of open-market operations is to reduce or to increase the cash reserves of the commercial banks held at the Bank of England, thereby compelling them to reduce or to increase their lending, and therefore the level of bank deposits. To reduce the quantity of money the Bank of England would sell securities on the stock exchange, payment being made by cheques drawn on the commercial banks. At the Clearing House all these cheques would require payment to be made to the Bank of England, and this would be accomplished by reducing the balances of the commercial banks at the Bank of England. Since the commercial banks regarded these balances as cash, their cash ratio would fall, and this would necessitate a reduction of bank deposits by curtailing their lending. To increase the quantity of money the Bank of England would buy securities in the market and set in motion a reverse train of events.

(c) *The Treasury Directive*. First employed in 1951, this takes the form of direct instructions to banks, usually to restrict their lending.

(d) *Special deposits*. In 1960, special deposits were introduced as an alternative to open-market operations. In order to reduce their cash ratio the commercial banks can be asked to make special deposits of a specified amount at the Bank of England. An increase, therefore, in special deposits will require the commercial banks to reduce their deposits by curtailing their lending. Special deposits can be released only when the monetary authorities agree to this course.

(e) *Adjuncts to monetary policy*. For a number of years monetary policy was supplemented by (i) fiscal policy, and (ii) variations in hire-purchase regulations. To check demand the Chancellor of the Exchequer would budget for a large surplus, mainly by increasing indirect taxes. To stimulate demand he would reduce taxation. At the same time hire-purchase regulations would be stiffened to make hire-purchase less attractive if demand was to be checked, or the regulations could be eased if the aim was to stimulate demand. Because hire-purchase changes severely affect only a limited range of goods this practice was discontinued.

QUESTIONS

1. Indicate the essential differences between the position of the Bank of England and that of the commercial banks, and explain carefully the relations between the Bank of England and the other financial institutions in this country. (R.S.A.)

2. What do you mean by open-market operations, and within what limits may they be employed? (I.B.)

3. What controls does the Bank of England exercise over the activities of the commercial banks in the United Kingdom? (G.C.E. Adv.)

4. What is the relationship of the Bank of England to the commercial banks? How, and for what purpose, does

the Bank of England control the activities of the commercial banks? (G.C.E. Ord.)

5. What is the importance of bank rate today?

6. What are the main functions of the Bank of England? (G.C.E. Adv.)

XXV. The Capital Market

1. What is the capital market?

Whereas the money market is the market for very short-term loans, the capital market is the market for longer-term loans—moderately short, medium, long and very long period and permanent loans. The demand to borrow capital comes mainly from industry and commerce, the Government, local authorities and sometimes from individuals.

2. The financing of industry

The capital market is the principal source of capital for industry and commerce.

(a) *Circulating capital.* In Great Britain firms often obtain their circulating capital from the commercial banks, which prefer to lend for relatively short periods, though bank loans are usually renewable. Bank loans can be supplemented by credit from suppliers, wholesalers assisting many retailers in this way.

(b) *Fixed capital.* It is rare for British banks to provide fixed capital for industry. The sole proprietor will have to depend on his own savings or possibly loans from friends or relatives. A new company will issue shares to the capital market either directly or through an issuing house. An existing company may increase its fixed capital by an issue of debentures or a further issue of shares. If the existing shareholders are given the first chance of taking up the new shares it is known as a "rights" issue. Many firms expand by "ploughing back" some of their profits into the business. When the capital of a limited company has been increased in this way bonus shares may be issued to the shareholders in proportion to the number of shares already held.

3. The supply of capital

The supply of capital to the capital market comes from the banks and the savings of individuals and institutions:

(a) *The commercial banks.* These provide businesses with short-term credit.

(b) *Individuals.* Many people subscribe directly to new issues of debentures, preference shares, and ordinary shares of public limited companies. Individuals can also subscribe directly for new issues of stocks put on the market by, or on behalf of, the Government or the larger local authorities. In all these cases the provision of capital gives rise to securities which can be bought and sold on the stock exchange. In addition, the Government borrows from individuals by issuing Savings Certificates, Savings Bonds and Premium Bonds, purchasable at banks and post offices.

(c) *Undistributed profits.* Corporate saving occurs when businesses finance themselves out of their undistributed profits, the company providing itself with additional fixed capital out of its own savings.

(d) *Insurance companies.* Through premiums paid to insurance companies individuals indirectly provide funds to the capital market, the insurance companies investing their funds in Government stocks, debentures and ordinary and preference shares.

(e) *Unit investment trusts and investment trust companies.* These are institutions through which the individual small investor can supply capital to industry with greater safety for himself by being able to spread even a small investment over a large number of companies. The unit trust has become popular with small investors, partly because it enables them to spread the risk, and partly because of the ease with which units can be bought and sold, generally direct from the managers of the trust. In the case of the investment company shares have to be obtained on the stock exchange, as with any other sort of company. In both cases the managers use the funds at their disposal to purchase shares in a number of companies—sometimes over one hundred.

(*f*) *Building societies*. Individuals can put money in building societies, which then in their turn they can lend to people who wish to buy property, mainly houses.

(*g*) *Finance companies and secondary banks*. These institutions help to finance hire-purchase transactions. They obtain their funds partly by borrowing from the commercial banks and partly from deposits obtained direct from individuals.

4. The provision of medium-term credit

The need of many firms for credit for periods intermediate between long and short term led to the establishment of special institutions to supply it. In 1974 these were merged as Finance for Industry (F.F.I.), the capital being provided by the Bank of England, the English and Scottish commercial banks, investment trusts and insurance companies. A great deal of assistance has been given to private limited companies.

5. The stock exchange

The capital market exists for the raising of new capital, whereas the stock exchange provides a market in existing securities. The capital market is wide in extent—in some cases world-wide—but the stock exchange carries on its business at a particular place. It is thus a good example of a highly-organised market. It is a place where stocks and shares can be bought or sold—that is, it is a market for old securities. There is a very important link between the capital market and the stock exchange. The ease with which stocks and shares can be sold on the stock exchange encourages investment in securities. So the stock exchange aids the flow of capital to productive industry, for it gives a degree of liquidity to securities which they would not otherwise possess.

The prices of stocks and shares on the stock exchange depend upon: (*i*) the prevailing rate of interest; (*ii*) the expected yield of the securities; (*iii*) the date of maturity where the stock is redeemable at a fixed date.

6. Method of doing business on the stock exchange

The chief members of the London Stock Exchange are brokers, who act as agents for investors and jobbers, who deal only with brokers. If an investor wishes to buy or sell a security he will instruct a broker to act for him, or he may authorise his bank to do so. Jobbers specialise in particular groups of stocks—gilt-edged, shares in banks, drapery and stores, engineering, gold mines, etc.—and so the broker will approach a jobber specialising in the kind of stock that he wishes to buy or sell. The broker will ask the jobber to quote a price for this stock, but when giving his quotation the jobber will not know whether the broker wishes to buy or to sell. He will name two prices, the higher being his selling price and the lower his buying price. Business on the stock exchange is conducted according to strict rules, and the jobber is compelled to deal at the prices he quotes.

7. Speculation

Many people buy stocks or shares for the purpose of investment, and having done so generally hold them for long periods. Some people, however, merely buy shares in the hope of being able to sell them again later at a profit. These are speculators. Those who buy in the hope that prices will rise are known as "bulls", while those who sell because they expect prices to fall are known as "bears". There are, however, both good and bad aspects of speculation: (i) some speculation tends to steady prices, since the speculators tend to buy when others are selling, and to sell when others wish to buy; but (ii) there can be bad results of speculation when the actions of the speculators themselves are directed towards influencing prices of securities. On many occasions suggestions have been put forward for reducing or eliminating "bad" speculation on the stock exchange. However, it is not always possible to distinguish between speculation and genuine investment, and the two motives themselves may often be inextricably mixed. The presence of speculators in the market makes possible, too, the buying or selling of securities at any time; without speculation securities would be less liquid.

QUESTIONS

1. What are the methods by which business firms normally finance their activities? (C.I.S. Final.)

2. Describe the various types of securities which are bought and sold on the stock exchange. (G.C.E. Ord.)

3. Describe how (a) a private firm, (b) a joint-stock company, may raise additional capital. (G.C.E. Ord.)

4. Examine the functions of the stock exchange. (G.C.E. Adv.)

XXVI. Fluctuations in Employment

1. Industrial fluctuations
Fluctuations in industrial production and employment fall into three clearly defined periods:

(a) the pre-1914 trade cycle which had persisted throughout the nineteenth century, with alternating brief periods of trade boom and depression;

(b) the inter-War years, 1919–39, a period of almost continuously high unemployment, including the Great Depression of 1929–35. This was the longest and most severe depression experienced in Great Britain.

(c) the post-1945 years, (i) to 1970, a period of mainly full or over-full employment, with minor recessions, and (ii) 1970–77, a period of increasing unemployment.

2. Features of the trade cycle
The pre-1914 trade cycle had the following features:

(a) down to 1914 depressions and booms alternated with one another at intervals of about seven or eight years;

(b) prices, production and the level of employment rose or fell together;

(c) there was no appreciable rise in retail prices until full employment was reached, but after that, prices rose because further expansion of production was not possible;

(d) greater fluctuations occurred in the production of producers' goods, the onset of a boom or depression being felt first in these industries;

(e) an expansion of credit occurred in a boom and a contraction of credit in a depression;

(f) there was less unemployment but more widespread distress due to low incomes in agriculture than in industrial occupations.

3. Theories of the trade cycle

Various explanations have been offered to explain the trade cycle, the truth probably being that there were many causes.

(a) *Real causes*. (i) Fluctuations in output occur where supply is slow to adjust itself to changes of demand, as in agriculture. (ii) The output of capital goods varies considerably between one year and another. Some writers attach little importance to real causes.

(b) *Psychological causes*. According to this view, the upswing or downswing of the trade cycle depends upon the confidence of business men in the future. If they expect rising prices to continue they are encouraged to expand production. After a time a fear of falling prices makes them curtail production and the boom is checked.

(c) *Purely monetary causes*. Banks, it is said, tend periodically to issue an excess of credit due to: (i) competition between banks in granting loans, and (ii) the fact that advances form a bank's most profitable asset. Expansion and contraction of bank credit, however, are more likely to be the result than the cause of business fluctuations.

(d) *Under-consumption as a cause*. A number of under-consumption theories have been put forward, all of which assert that the purchasing power of consumers is insufficient to buy the quantity of goods produced. It was thought that purchasing power was lost in some way because costs incurred in production did not give rise to an equal amount of purchasing power in the hands of consumers, this tendency being aggravated by the withdrawal of purchasing power in consequence of saving. Supporters of the cruder versions of this theory proposed as the remedy periodic gifts of money to consumers. The weakness of under-consumption theories is that consumers' purchasing power is not permanently insufficient to purchase the goods produced. All expenses of production became income to some people.

(e) *The saving–investment theory*. Demand, and, therefore, consumption depends on the level of income, and this in its turn depends on real investment, that is, the production of capital goods. Saving, that is, abstention from the purchase of consumers' goods, is a pre-requisite of investment, and if there is too little investment there will be unemployment. To achieve full employment investment must be adequate. Saving, investment and consumption, therefore, depend on one another, and together determine the level of total income. Figure 13 shows how investment, saving and consumption influence one another and the level of income and employment.

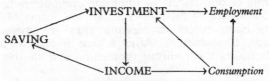

FIG. 13—*Influences on Employment and Consumption.*

Some writers believe that if saving exceeds investment there will be unemployment, but if investment exceeds saving the demand for labour will exceed the supply, but according to Lord Keynes saving and investment are always equal. Nowadays this is taken to mean that the investment of one period determines the saving of the next period.

(f) *The multiplier*. A given amount of investment will create a greater amount of employment than that directly resulting from it. For example, if a new project requires 1,000 men the extra demand arising from their increased incomes will increase the demand for labour, so that perhaps altogether 3,000 additional men may be employed. In this case the multiplier would be 3.

4. Full employment

Since 1944 the British Government has accepted responsibility for full employment. About the same time Lord

Beveridge published his book *Full Employment in a Free Society*, in which he outlined proposals for the maintenance of full employment. This requires:

(*a*) a high level of demand for which there must be adequate investment. Therefore, if private investment falls short of the required amount the State should supplement it with public investment;

(*b*) that the location of industry should be controlled;

(*c*) that labour should be mobile;

(*d*) that trade unions should adopt a responsible attitude to the problem of wages, since full employment puts them in a strong bargaining position and increases in wages in excess of increases in production can only result in inflation.

If an excessive amount of investment is undertaken a condition of overfull employment will occur, in which the demand for labour will exceed the supply—an inflationary situation. For a country such as Great Britain with a great export trade the maintenance of full employment depends also on the level of employment in other countries.

Problems of full employment. The maintenance of full employment brings its own problems:

(*a*) The danger of inflation is increased as a result of the tendency for investment to be excessive.

(*b*) The danger of inflation will also be increased because full employment puts trade unions in a strong bargaining position, and rises in wages stimulate the inflationary spiral of wages and prices.

(*c*) Labour tends to be unevenly distributed, so that shortages of labour occur in some areas with unemployment in others.

From 1945 to 1970, full employment was generally maintained in Great Britain, except during sterling crises associated with balance of payments difficulties when deflationary policies had to be pursued. For over twenty years until 1967 the unemployment rate was below 2%, and for much of the time it only slightly exceeded 1%.

After 1970 unemployment rose almost continuously, by 1977 reaching a total of one and a half million.

Thus, unemployment became more serious than had been expected, full employment, however, being sacrificed to other needs of the economy—the attempt to prevent the devaluation of 1967, the necessity to secure large surpluses in the balance of payments during 1968–71 in order to increase the rate of economic growth.

One serious aspect of unemployment in recent times has been its uneven distribution, first during the Great Depression of 1929–35 and again, since 1960, unemployment in the development areas—Wales, North-east England, Scotland and Northern Ireland—being much worse than elsewhere, with little unemployment at any time in South-east England.

QUESTIONS

1. Investigate the statement that cyclical fluctuations are more pronounced in industries producing capital goods and durable consumption goods than in others.

2. What is the trade cycle? Give one explanation offered by economists. (G.C.E. Adv.)

3. Describe briefly the main features of the trade cycle. (C.I.S. Final.)

4. What do you know of (a) the trade cycle, (b) any remedies suggested for its cure? (A.C.A. Final.)

XXVII. International Trade and the Balance of Payments

1. International division of labour

Differences of climate, soil, etc., result in the production of different commodities in different parts of the world. International trade owes its origin to this fact, and every country taking part in it can thus enjoy a wider range of commodities. Nowadays, however, many countries import goods that they could produce themselves, for countries tend to specialise in the production of those goods for which they have the greatest comparative advantage over other countries. So Great Britain grows less wheat than it could and prefers to specialise in manufacturing. This is the *Principle of Comparative Cost* and is the basis of all international trade. This theory was first developed by Ricardo.

2. Advantages of international trade

The Principle of Comparative Cost can best be illustrated by examples. It is usual to assume a simple case where only two countries take part and there are only two entering into articles of trade. Let the two countries be Utopia and Ruritania and let the two commodities be wheat and rice.

(a) Suppose that for a given cost of production Utopia can produce either 100 units of wheat or 50 units of rice and Ruritania 50 units of wheat or 100 units of rice. Then without specialisation total production will be:

	Units of wheat		Units of rice
Utopia	100	+	50
Ruritania	50	+	100
Total	150	+	150

If now each specialises in the production of the commodity for which it has a comparative advantage over the other total production will be:

	Units of wheat		Units of rice
Utopia	200	+	0
Ruritania	0	+	200
Total	200	+	200

By specialisation there is thus an increase of 50 units in the output of each commodity. If an exchange of 60 units of wheat for 60 units of rice took place the stocks held by these two countries would be:

	Units of wheat		Units of rice
Utopia	140	+	60
Ruritania	60	+	140
Total	200	+	200

As a result of exchange each country will have a bigger supply of each commodity. International trade, therefore, benefits both countries.

(b) Even if Utopia can produce both commodities more cheaply than Ruritania, it would still be an advantage to both to introduce specialisation, if (say) Utopia had a greater advantage over Ruritania in the production of (say) wheat. Suppose that for a given cost of production Utopia can produce 100 units of wheat or 100 units of rice and Ruritania 40 units of wheat or 80 units of rice. Then without specialisation total production will be:

	Units of wheat		Units of rice
Utopia	100	+	100
Ruritania	40	+	80
Total	140	+	180

If Utopia specialises in wheat production, although continuing to produce a little rice, while Ruritania specialises in the production of rice total production will then be:

	Units of wheat		Units of rice
Utopia	160	+	40
Ruritania	0	+	160
Total	160	+	200

Again, as a result of specialisation there is an increased output of each commodity—an extra 20 units of both wheat and rice. If Utopia exchanges (say) 50 units of wheat for (say) 70 units of rice the position will then be:

	Units of wheat		Units of rice
Utopia	110	+	110
Ruritania	50	+	90
Total	160	+	200

As a result of the exchange each country has ten more units of each commodity than it would have had if there had been no specialisation and no international trade.

Terms of trade. The rate of exchange between wheat and rice in the above examples will depend upon the relative strength of demand of each country for the commodity produced by the other. This is known as the terms of trade. In actual conditions a country's terms of trade depend on the relative prices of its imports and its exports, the terms of trade being said to be favourable when the prices of its exports rise relatively to the prices of its imports.

3. Barriers to international specialisation
In practice there are obstacles to the free working of the Principle of Comparative Cost:

(*a*) Government interference, e.g. by the introduction of import quotas, by duties on imports, bounties on export and exchange control.

(*b*) Lack of mobility of factors of production, especially labour, in both occupational and geographical senses.

(*c*) The existence of different national currencies and banking systems complicates international transactions.

4. The balance of payments

By the balance of payments is meant the relation between the payments of all kinds made from one country to the rest of the world and its receipts from other countries. Payments are mainly for goods imported from abroad, and receipts come chiefly from the export of goods to other countries. At one time each country used to strive for a "favourable" balance of trade, that is an excess of exports over imports. Since, however, the exports of one country form the imports of another, for the world as a whole imports must equal exports. The relation between a country's imports and its exports is its balance of trade (or invisible balance).

The visible balance, however, forms only part of the balance of payments which is also influenced by a number of "invisible" items. When allowance is made for both visible and invisible items this yields the balance of payments on current account.

Capital movements also give rise to payments and receipts whether due to (a) investment abroad, or (b) speculative activity. When these are taken into account the result is the balance of payments on capital account. When total receipts exceed total payments this is known as a *favourable* or *active* balance, and when payments exceed receipts there is said to be an *unfavourable* or *passive* balance.

5. Invisible items

These arise in connection with payments for or receipts from services. For a long time Great Britain has had a considerable income from its invisible exports, with the result that this country has been able to have an excess of imports of goods over exports of goods. The chief invisible items in the British balance of payments are:

(a) *Transport by sea and air*. At one time this was a very important source of income from abroad, but with the decline of transport by sea, Great Britain no longer enjoys the large share of the world's carrying trade as formerly.

(*b*) *Interest and dividends from investments abroad*. This item is still very much in Great Britain's favour, though recently there has been a large increase in foreign investment in Great Britain.

(*c*) *Financial services*. Profits accruing to London as a world centre for banking, insurance and other financial services.

(*d*) *Travel*. Expenditure of tourists and other travellers. Nowadays this is often for Great Britain a self-balancing item.

(*e*) *Government expenditure abroad*. This may occur as a result of (*i*) military commitments or (*ii*) assistance to developing countries.

6. Methods of correcting an adverse balance of payments

There are a number of ways by which an adverse balance of payments can be corrected. Some of the methods that have been employed are:

(*a*) *Deflation*. This results in a reduction of money incomes and prices through a curtailment of the money supply. As a result, exports are stimulated because they are now cheaper to people living in other countries, and imports are checked because they are now dearer to people in the home country who have less money to spend.

(*b*) *Devaluation of the currency*. This reduces the value of the home currency in terms of others. As a result imports are dearer and so tend to be reduced, and exports are cheaper to other peoples and so will tend to increase.

(*c*) *Exchange depreciation*. This means allowing a currency to fall in value on the foreign exchange in terms of other currencies, the result being that exports become cheaper to foreigners and imports dearer in the home market.

(*d*) *Exchange control*. This may take the form of Government intervention on the foreign exchange market or the restriction of purchases of foreign currency by its own people. This course is open to a country with a fixed rate of exchange and unwilling to devalue its currency. The success of this type of policy depends on a country's resources of foreign currency.

(e) Restriction of imports by *tariffs*, temporary *surcharges on imports* or *import quotas*.

These methods are considered in more detail in XXIX to XXXI.

It is said that a balance of payments must always balance. This merely means that a debit (or credit) balance must be covered in some way. This can be done in one of the following ways:

(a) by an export of gold when the currency is linked to gold.
(b) by drawing on the International Monetary Fund;
(c) by borrowing from another country;
(d) by obtaining imports on credit;
(e) by selling some of its foreign investments.

Most of these methods make things more difficult for the country in the future. The years 1964–67 were particularly difficult for sterling, with an adverse balance of payments each year until the devaluation of the pound in 1967. Although in most years before 1967 Great Britain had a favourable balance of payments, the position has often been felt to be precarious because of the country's inadequate reserves. Then followed a series of years with large surpluses. In 1972 the position was very near to balance. There followed another period of great difficulty with the balance of payments, aggravated by the action of the oil producing countries (OPEC) in combining to raise the price of oil. As a result, unprecedented deficits occurred during 1975–77. The development of North Sea oil should greatly ease Great Britain's balance of payments problem.

7. The British balance of payments
Table XI shows the chief items in the British balance of payments on current account.

TABLE XI. *British Balance of Payments.*

	1972		1976	
Payments (£ million):				
Imports (goods)		10,151		28,897
Invisible items:				
Government expenditure abroad	423		969	
Sea transport and civil aviation	2,021		4,016	
Interest and dividends	1,198		2,167	
Travel	527		1,008	
Other items	1,085	5,254	3,512	11,672
Total payments		15,405		40,569
Receipts (£ million):				
Exports (goods)		9,449		25,416
Invisible items:				
Sea transport and civil aviation	2,023		4,302	
Interest and dividends	492		3,746	
Financial services	1,742		1,086	
Travel	546		1,628	
Other items	1,258	6,061	3,076	13,838
Total receipts		15,510		39,254
Balance		+ 105		− 1,315

+ = Credit balance   − = Debit balance

QUESTIONS

1. "Exports pay for imports." How far is this true? (G.C.E. Ord.)

2. Explain as briefly as you can the main outlines of the Theory of International Trade. (A.C.A. Final.)

3. What are the advantages and disadvantages of international division of labour? (G.C.E. Ord.)

4. Why is it that Great Britain imports certain foodstuffs which could be grown in Britain? (G.C.E. Ord.)

5. What is meant by the balance of payments? Why does it balance? (G.C.E. Adv.)

6. What economic frictions hamper the free play of supply and demand in international trade? (I.B.)

XXVIII. Free Trade and Protection

1. Free trade
In the late nineteenth century and down to 1914, Great Britain approached most nearly of all countries in the world to free trade. The period 1860–70 saw most countries come nearer to free trade than ever before. More correctly this was a period of low duties. After 1871 there was a reaction in favour of higher tariffs. Following the war of 1914–18 many of the new countries of Europe attempted to become self-sufficient behind tariff barriers, while the Great Depression of 1929–35 led to a general raising of tariffs throughout the world. Although duties had previously been imposed on foreign pianos, motor cars, etc., Great Britain did not really abandon its traditional free-trade policy until 1932.

2. Arguments in favour of protection
Many arguments have been put forward in support of a policy of protection:

(a) *Infant industries*. Protection is often sought for newly-established industries, which in their early stages of development are unable to withstand foreign competition. When such industries have become mature the duties should be removed, but experience shows that "infant" industries never seem to grow up.

(b) *To restore an adverse balance of payments*. An excess of imports may be checked by the imposition of import duties, but it is probable that exports also will be reduced. The efficacy of a tariff for this purpose is therefore very doubtful.

(c) *To secure greater stability of foreign trade*. There is little to substantiate this argument. Tariffs are usually subject to periodic revision, and this creates uncertainty.

(d) *Dumping*. This may occur under monopoly. Protection may be demanded for either of two purposes: (i) to the home market from foreign competition; or (ii) to protect the home market against the dumping of goods by a foreign monopolist.

(e) *To protect the standard of living*. This argument has often been put forward in countries where high wages prevail. Foreign countries with cheap labour, it is said, compete unfairly in the home market. In any case such protection can be applied only to the home market, and labour producing for foreign markets cannot be protected in this way.

(f) *Self-sufficiency*. In order to enable a country to provide for all its basic needs, particularly in time of war, industries otherwise incapable of withstanding foreign competition are developed under the protection of a tariff.

(g) *As a bargaining weapon*. Duties may be imposed as a retaliatory measure against countries with high tariffs. These can then be used as a bargaining weapon in any discussion on the reduction of duties.

(h) *As an emergency measure*. In an extreme depression, such as that of 1929–35, a tariff may offer some slight advantage if the harm done by it to the export industries is less than the benefit accruing to industries producing for the home market.

3. Arguments against protection
The arguments against protection are much stronger:

(a) It is contrary to the Principle of Comparative Cost. If this principle is not carried out it means that countries are failing to take advantage of specialisation, so that the total output of the world as a whole will be less than it might be. Protection diverts resources to less-productive uses.

(b) To restrict imports means in the long run a restriction of exports. For example, unless a country earns foreign currency it cannot buy foreign goods.

(c) Once duties have been imposed for a particular purpose it is difficult to obtain their removal.

(d) The imposition or raising of tariffs leads to reprisals and a general increase of tariffs all round, with a consequent reduction in the volume of international trade.

(e) Tariffs raise the level of costs in relation to other countries, and thus raise the cost of living.

4. Import quotas

These fix the maximum physical amount of a commodity that can be imported during a particular period. Import licences are then issued to the countries supplying the commodity, and these state the maximum amount each country is permitted to supply.

The chief *advantage* of this system is that home producers know exactly how much of certain commodities is to be imported.

The chief *disadvantages* of the system are:

(a) as compared with import duties there is a loss of revenue;

(b) the consumers of the country imposing the import quotas do not benefit from falling prices on the world market, the importers receiving the difference between the world price and the home price;

(c) bi-lateral trade is encouraged, whereas for the free working of the Principle of Comparative Cost multilateral trade is required.

5. Export duties

As long ago as 1828 Huskisson abolished duties on exports from Great Britain. Since such duties tend to check exports, they are rarely imposed nowadays. Only where there is a very inelastic foreign demand for the commodity is it advantageous for a country to tax its exports. India, for example, imposes export duties on tea.

6. Regional free trade

Attempts have been made since 1945 to develop regional areas of free trade. In 1947 Belgium, Holland and Luxembourg formed Benelux. In 1952, these three combined with France, West Germany and Italy to form the European Coal and Steel Community. The Treaty of Rome (1957) established the European Economic Community (EEC), better known in Great Britain as the Common Market. These countries gradually reduced tariffs, so that by 1969 they comprised an area of free trade.

Shortly afterwards, a second regional area of free trade was established in Europe, known as the European Free Trade Area (EFTA), consisting of Great Britain, Norway, Sweden, Denmark, Switzerland, Austria and Portugal.

Great Britain wished to join the EEC, but it was necessary to protect the interests of New Zealand and the developing countries of the Commonwealth. There were prolonged negotiations in 1962–63, and again in 1967, between Great Britain and the EEC countries, but it was not until 1971 that the EEC accepted Great Britain's application for admission. At the same time Denmark and the Republic of Ireland were admitted to the EEC. In 1975 a referendum confirmed Great Britain's membership. In 1977 further applications for membership were made by Portugal, Spain and Greece.

The wider the area of free trade, the greater the possibilities of specialisation, and therefore the greater the total output of the whole area and the wider the market for each country's products. All the members of such organisations are therefore likely to benefit, some industries very greatly, though some others may suffer.

It is hoped that, eventually, Great Britain's economic growth will accelerate as result of its becoming a member of the EEC. A drawback, however, to membership of the EEC has been the necessity to accept the Community's agricultural policy, the effect of which has been to increase food prices in Great Britain. Members of the Commonwealth in Africa and the Caribbean became associate members of the EEC on the same terms as the former French colonies.

7. GATT

The General Agreement on Tariffs and Trade (GATT), with headquarters in Geneva, was established in 1947 with the aim of reducing tariffs throughout the world. A number of international conferences have been held since then and tariffs have been considerably reduced. Even greater reductions were agreed in 1967 in what was known as the Kennedy Round, on account of its having been initiated by the late President Kennedy of the United States.

QUESTIONS

1. The principal weapon employed to regulate foreign trade is the tariff. What other methods have come into common use in the present century? (C.I.S. Final.)

2. Discuss the probable effects of a reduction in the import duty on motor-cars. (G.C.E. Adv.)

3. Discuss the case of using tariffs to exclude the importation of goods produced in countries where wages are low.

4. Consider the effects of the formation of a customs union upon the economies of its member states.

XXIX. Foreign Exchange:
(i) The Gold Standard

1. Features of the gold standard
When a country is on the full gold standard the standard unit of its currency contains a fixed amount in gold, and the price of gold is fixed by law. The gold sovereign which circulated in Great Britain down to 1914 consisted of gold 11/12 fine at £3 17s. 9d. (about £3.89) per fine oz. Thus, the sovereign contained an amount of gold worth exactly the face value of the coin. Bank of England notes were exchangeable on demand for gold. There were no restrictions on the import or export of gold. A gold reserve had to be kept sufficient to meet all demands for it.

The chief advantage of the gold standard was that it provided stable exchange rates between countries on it, for the relative values of the coins of different countries could easily be calculated by comparing the gold content of the various coinages. This is the mint par of exchange. The rate of exchange between two countries on the gold standard could vary from this only by the cost of the transport of gold between the two centres.

2. Specie points
If the rate of exchange between sterling and (say) French francs fell below the cost of transport and insurance it would be cheaper for the British merchant to send gold in payment. The rate of exchange could not, therefore, fall below this level. Again, a French merchant, with a debt payment in Great Britain, would not pay for sterling more than the mint par of exchange + the cost of transport and insurance. The rate of exchange could not, therefore, rise above this level. These two extreme points of variation in the rate of exchange were known as "specie points" or "gold points".

3. Types of gold standard

Several forms of the gold standard have been operated:

(a) *The full gold standard*. In this case gold coins circulate and on demand bank-notes can be exchanged for an equivalent amount in gold. This type of gold standard operated in Great Britain down to 1914.

(b) *The gold bullion standard*. Under this system individual bank-notes are not convertible into gold on demand. When Great Britain adopted this form of the gold standard during 1925–31 the Bank of England would exchange gold bars of 400 oz. each for an equivalent value in notes. Owing to the softness of the metal, a gold coinage is expensive to maintain, and so one advantage of the gold bullion standard is that it economises the use of gold.

(c) *The gold exchange standard*. On this form of the gold standard the central bank will exchange on demand its country's currency, not for gold, but for the currency of some other country on the gold standard. Between 1925 and 1931 the Scandinavian countries adopted this form of gold standard, and this meant that their central banks had to keep reserves of sterling. Countries adopting a gold exchange standard are dependent upon the monetary policy of the "parent" country, for example, when Great Britain left the gold standard in 1931 those countries found that their sterling assets fell in value.

4. The working of the gold standard

The gold standard performs two functions. Not only does it serve as an internal standard but it also has an important influence on international transactions and the balance of payments.

(a) *An internal standard*. Since the price of gold is fixed, changes in its value can be brought about only by changes in the prices of other commodities. On the gold standard how much money a country has depends on its stock of gold, which directly determines the quantity of cash and indirectly the volume of bank deposits.

(b) *An international standard.* The chief advantage of an international gold standard is that it provides stability of exchange rates, for fluctuating rates handicap trade. An excess of imports will cause an outflow of gold, and since this reduces the quantity of money in the country by an equivalent amount, prices fall. This makes imports relatively dearer, and so imports are checked, while at the same time, home-produced goods become cheaper, and so exports are encouraged. Thus an adverse balance of payments is said to be automatically corrected. Similarly, an excess of exports produces an inflow of gold from abroad, increasing the quantity of money, causing prices to rise, and thus encouraging imports and checking exports. If, however, it happens that the outflow of gold cannot be checked the country will be forced off the gold standard, which can be maintained only if the movement of gold is not too great or too prolonged.

(c) *Interaction of the gold standard at home and abroad.* A country on the gold standard cannot, therefore, adopt an independent monetary policy, its internal monetary policy being dependent on its balance of payments. The central bank must take measures to protect the gold reserve if there is an outflow of gold. It will be necessary to adopt a deflationary monetary policy, interest rates being raised and supported by open-market operations. These actions of the central bank will reduce the reserves of the commercial banks, which, to maintain their cash ratio, must contract credit. Thus the quantity of money in the country is reduced. In the case of an inflow of gold, interest will be lowered, the central bank buying securities in the open market, in order to bring about an expansion of credit. The so-called "rules of the gold standard" therefore are that the quantity of money should be reduced when gold is flowing out of the country and increased when gold is flowing in. Internal monetary policy thus becomes dependent upon the inflow or outflow of gold. The gold standard may require an expansion or contraction of credit at times when the internal situation demands the opposite policy.

Advantages of the gold standard: (i) it ensures a stable

rate of exchange; (*ii*) the danger of a "runaway" inflation is removed so long as a country can stay on the gold standard; (*iii*) the balance of payments is "automatically" brought into balance.

Disadvantages: internal monetary policy depends directly on whether the balance of payments results in an outflow or inflow of gold, so that the monetary policy most appropriate to the internal situation cannot always be adopted. This is regarded as the main disadvantage of the gold standard.

5. Causes of gold flows

When a country is on the gold standard an inflow or outflow of gold may take place for one of the following reasons:

(*a*) *An adverse balance of payments on current account.* An excess of imports over exports in the balance of trade, unless offset by a favourable balance in invisible items, will have to be covered by an export of gold. In the opposite case, an overall favourable balance will result in gold being imported.

(*b*) *Capital movements.* An export of capital has a similar effect to an excess of imports, and will cause an outflow of gold. Investment abroad should, therefore, be undertaken only when a country has a favourable balance of payments on current account as an alternative to accumulating excessive gold reserves. Great Britain built up its foreign investment in the nineteenth century as a result of its favourable balance of trade at that time. Long-term capital movements aid the economic development of under-developed countries. Short-term capital movements of a speculative nature only cause difficulties with their balances of payments.

(*c*) *Monetary policy.* If a country on the gold standard attempts to inflate to a greater extent than other countries it will suffer an outflow of gold. The gold standard, however, does not prevent inflation; all countries on the gold standard can inflate together, if they all inflate to the same extent.

6. Devaluation

A country, desirous of maintaining a stable rate of exchange, may decide to remain on the gold standard, but at a lower gold parity. Devaluation may enable a country to avoid deflation, which is unpopular. The value of its currency in terms of others will then be reduced, and this will stimulate exports, which will then be cheaper to foreign buyers, and check imports, which will have become dearer to home buyers. Devaluation may provide relief in a crisis, but if there is fear of further devaluation other countries will lose confidence in the currency. If other countries devalue their currencies any advantage of devaluation will be lost, and competitive devaluation, therefore, is to be avoided, since, if carried to excess, it can only result in currencies becoming worthless. Sterling was devalued in 1949 from $4.03 to $2.80 to the £ and again in 1967 from $2.80 to $2.40 to the £.

The effect of devaluation will be short-lived if the higher prices of imported food and raw materials lead to increases in wages, thereby increasing the cost of home-produced goods and so checking foreign demand for them.

7. The breakdown of the gold standard

In 1931 Great Britain and some other countries left the gold standard. Others followed. Some of the chief causes of the breakdown of the gold standard were:

(a) Not carrying out the "rules" of the gold standard to deflate when there was an outflow of gold and to inflate when gold was flowing in. Deflation was unpopular because: (i) it checks production, and (ii) it is likely to cause unemployment.

(b) The over-valuation of sterling when Great Britain returned to the gold standard in 1925. This required an excessive amount of deflation.

(c) Short-term capital movements. A mass of short-term funds, known as "hot money", moved from one centre to another for speculative reasons, generally seeking safety rather than a higher rate of interest.

QUESTIONS

1. How would you account for the world-wide failure of the gold standard between the two world wars? (I.B.)

2. What do you understand by the "rules of the gold standard"? (C.I.S. Final.)

3. What do you mean by the gold standard? What was the difference between the gold standard of 1913 and that of 1925–31? (A.I.B. Pt. 1.)

4. What do you understand by the gold standard? What are the essential features of such an arrangement? (G.C.E. Ord.)

5. When can devaluation help a country's balance of payments?

XXX. Foreign Exchange: (ii) Off the Gold Standard

1. Flexible (or floating) exchange rates

The gold standard was suspended in the war of 1914–18, during which exchange rates were fixed; between 1919 and 1925 exchange rates were free to fluctuate. Exchange control was introduced on Great Britain's leaving the gold standard in 1931. During the Second World War there were again fixed exchange rates, as again under the IMF scheme which operated during 1945–72. Fixed exchange rates again gave way in 1972 to "floating" or freely fluctuating rates.

When exchange rates are perfectly free to fluctuate the rate of exchange depends upon the supply and demand for a currency on the foreign-exchange market. Speculation prevents a currency having a higher value in one centre than another, for should such a difference arise, speculators will buy currency in the cheaper centre and sell in the dearer. This type of speculation is known as arbitrage.

Advantage. A country can pursue an independent internal monetary policy, since this will no longer be determined by gold movements. Thus, it will never be necessary to adopt an unpopular deflationary policy.

Disadvantages. Instability of exchange rates increases the uncertainties of international trade. There is too a greater danger of a runaway inflation than with fixed exchange rates. There have been many serious inflations in periods when exchange rates were free to fluctuate, including that of the United Kingdom during 1975–77.

2. Depreciation

Under a system of flexible exchange rates an adverse balance of payments is automatically corrected by the depreciation of the currency in terms of others. For example, if Great Britain and the United States were the only two countries engaged in international trade the rate of exchange being (say) two dollars to £1, an excess of imports to Great Britain would result in an increase of sterling in the United States; and the price of sterling would fall, (say) to one and a half dollars to £1. As a result an American article priced at six dollars would increase in price in sterling from £3 to £4, this rise in price checking British imports. At the same time an article priced at £3 in Great Britain would fall in price in dollars from six to four and a half dollars, and this would stimulate American purchase of British exports. In this way the balance of payments would be restored.

The demand for foreign currency, however, does not depend only on the demand for imports from abroad. It can also be influenced by capital movements, speculation or even political considerations.

3. The purchasing power parity theory

This theory, refined by Cassel, was put forward to explain the rate of exchange when currencies are free to fluctuate. It asserts that the rate of exchange between such currencies depends upon the relative purchasing power of the currencies in the countries concerned, changes in the price levels altering the rate of exchange.

Criticisms of the theory:

(*a*) It is very difficult to compare the purchasing power of money in different countries, owing to demand of different peoples not being for the same groups of commodities.

(*b*) The rate of exchange may fluctuate considerably without any change in relative purchasing power, as a result of capital movements.

(*c*) Changes in demand. An increased demand for a particular import will raise the value of the currency of the exporting country. In consequence, to the importing country *all* imports become dearer, whereas for the exporting country *all* its imports will be cheaper. Apart, however, from imports, the relative cost of living in the two countries will be unchanged.

(*d*) Political changes, e.g. a change of Government may influence rates of exchange.

4. Exchange control

On the breakdown of the gold standard in the 1930s there was no wish to return to flexible exchange rates on account of their association with the great inflations of the 1920s. Recourse, therefore, was had to exchange control. Three aims of exchange control can be distinguished:

(*a*) *To keep rates of exchange stable*. This became the British Government's policy after 1932.

(*b*) *Under-valuation* of a currency in order to stimulate exports. This may lead to reprisals by other countries in the form of tariffs, or it may result in competitive devaluation.

(*c*) *Over-valuation*. This will check exports on account of their higher prices and encourage imports which appear to be cheaper. Over-valuation may be a policy deliberately adopted after a great war, or at other times when an effort has to be made to maintain confidence in the currency.

5. Methods of exchange control

Instead of allowing the exchange rate for its currency to vary, a Government may adopt measures to control the rate:

(*a*) *Intervention*. In this case the Government itself enters the foreign-exchange market to buy or sell its own or foreign currency. The extent to which a Government can influence the exchange rate of its currency will depend on its resources of foreign currency.

(*b*) *Restriction*. In this case the Government restricts the amount of foreign currency its own people are permitted to acquire.

Thus, there are two main types of exchange control. During 1932–39 the British Government adopted an interventionist policy; after 1939 it went over to restriction but returned to intervention again later. Germany adopted a restrictionist policy in 1931.

6. Exchange equalisation accounts

Great Britain was the first country to establish an exchange equalisation account, France and the United States following later. The purpose of these accounts was to maintain a stable rate of exchange, and if possible to prevent purely speculative activity affecting the rate. The British account was set up as a department of the Treasury in 1932, with the Bank of England as its agent. Its initial resources were. newly issued Treasury bills. The time was opportune for there was a strong demand for sterling, which the British account could easily supply, and in exchange it obtained foreign currency, which it later exchanged for gold. When the supply of sterling in the market was considered to be too great the British account purchased some of it in exchange for other currencies in order to check a fall in the exchange rate.

The successful working of the account was dependent on the extent of the Treasury's resources of sterling and foreign currency, but since neither over nor under-valuation was the aim, this type of intervention was more practicable than some others.

At that time the rate of exchange between sterling and the U.S. dollar was allowed to fluctuate freely on the foreign-exchange market only between an upper and a lower unit. The British Exchange Equalisation Account intervened to prevent it from varying beyond these limits.

The British Exchange Equalisation Account thus became, along with the Bank of England, a second holder of gold in this country. By the transfer of gold from the bank to the account it became possible to "sterilise" gold—that is, to prevent it penetrating into the monetary system as, in fact, became the American practice. Upon the outbreak of war in 1939 most of the gold held by the bank was transferred to the Exchange Equalisation Account.

7. Restriction

During 1933–39 Germany had the most thorough system of exchange control. The German people were forbidden to acquire foreign currency, and any they possessed had to be sold to the Reichsbank, the German Central Bank. Foreigners also were forbidden to export German currency, their holdings being placed in *"blocked accounts"*. Foreign trade came to be almost entirely under the control of the Reichsbank. Not unnaturally, reprisals came from foreign countries, and trade with Germany was eventually almost reduced to barter. Restriction as a weapon of exchange control therefore resulted in the strangling of international trade. Germany was also the first country to introduce multiple exchange rates, the rate obtainable depending on the purpose for which the currency was wanted.

Since 1945 exchange control has been practised by many countries with varying degrees of restriction or intervention. Many countries, for example, from time to time have offered foreign tourists a more favourable rate of exchange. Great Britain has not really favoured this practice, but for many years the amount of foreign currency permitted to British people for holiday or other private purposes was severely restricted. Since 1959 Great Britain has had a minimum of exchange control, though Government intervention in the foreign-exchange market was retained.

QUESTIONS

1. State and examine the "purchasing power parity" theory of foreign exchange. Is it applicable under the gold standard? (I.B.)

2. Account for the existence, and describe the functions of Exchange Equalisation Accounts. Indicate in outline how the British account operated prior to 1939. (C.I.S. Final.)

3. Explain briefly the motives for, and methods of, exchange control. (C.I.S. Final.)

4. What is the *purchasing-power parity* theory? Do you

think it provides an adequate explanation of the price of one currency in terms of another when foreign-exchange markets are free? (G.C.E. Adv.)

5. Examine the factors that determine the rate at which one currency exchanges for another in a free foreign-exchange market. (G.C.E. Adv.)

XXXI. International Monetary Co-operation

1. The Bretton Woods agreement

During the years 1931–39 the volume of international trade was greatly reduced as a result of exchange control, high tariffs, discriminatory practices, bi-lateral trade agreements, multiple exchange rates, blocked accounts and restrictions on the acquisition of foreign currencies. In an attempt to prevent a return to these chaotic conditions a conference was held in 1944 at Bretton Woods in the United States. Its purpose was to devise a system of international exchange for use after the war that would maximise world trade. The aims were to:

(a) make all currencies freely convertible in order to encourage multi-lateral trade;

(b) keep exchange rates stable;

(c) provide some means of assisting a country with *temporary* difficulties with its balance of payments.

A return to the gold standard would have satisfied the first two conditions, but this was regarded as too rigid a system. A new scheme was therefore devised, involving the establishment of two new international institutions—the International Monetary Fund and the International (or World) Bank.

2. The International Monetary Fund

The chief features of the scheme were:

(a) *Rates of exchange.* The member countries had to declare the par values of their currencies by, in terms of gold (or in practice US dollars) an agreed date. The sterling–dollar parity was originally fixed at 4.03 dollars.

(b) *Changes of parity*. Members were not to change the values of their currencies without first consulting the Fund. Devaluation of a currency was permitted only in the case of a country with an adverse balance of payments.

(c) *Convertibility of currencies*. Eventually all currencies were to be freely convertible, but owing to the war there was to be a transition period of five years during which some measure of exchange control would be permitted.

(d) *The pool*. This was to consist of gold and member countries' currencies. Contributions were based on the quotas assigned to members. Of the quota, 75% could be paid in the member's own currency and the remainder in gold or gold and US dollars. The quotas (in millions of dollars) ranged from 2,750 for the United States and 1,300 for Great Britain to 450 for France and 50 for Norway. Quotas were increased in 1959 and again in 1965.

Each member was allowed to purchase from the Fund foreign currency in exchange for its own up to the amount of its quota, though not more than 25% of this could be taken in any one year. This made it possible for a country to have an adverse balance of payments for a limited amount and for a limited period, but any excess would have to be covered by gold. The new system was thus less rigid than the gold standard.

3. The International or World Bank

The capital International Bank was provided by Governments of member countries. Its aims were:

(a) to aid reconstruction after the war;

(b) to provide the growth of international trade;

(c) to encourage investment, but through the usual private channels.

The activities of the World Bank are now supplemented by two other international institutions—the International Finance Corporation (IFC) and the International Development Association (IDA).

4. Recent monetary history

Some of the main events in recent monetary history that have affected Great Britain are:

(a) *The Washington Agreement (1946)*. Under this agreement Great Britain obtained a loan from the United States conditionally on sterling being made freely convertible by July 1947.

(b) *The Convertibility Crisis (1947)*. When sterling became convertible, the strain on Great Britain's gold and dollar reserves proved to be too great, and convertibility of sterling had to be withdrawn. Too much haste was shown in putting the Bretton Woods Scheme into operation: Great Britain and other countries of Western Europe had suffered from the war to a much greater extent than had been realised.

(c) *The Marshall Plan*. This led the United States to introduce the Marshall Plan, under which the United States gave assistance to Great Britain and some other countries to the value of many thousand million dollars. Meanwhile, the activities of the IMF were suspended.

(d) *The devaluation of sterling (1949)*. The assistance permitted by the quotas that the IMF could give to a country in difficulties with its balances of payments proved to be totally inadequate for the needs in the difficult years after 1945. It was felt too, especially in the United States, that there was a fundamental disequilibrium in the British balance of payments that could be remedied only by a devaluation of the pound. In fact the par values of currencies had been arbitrarily fixed, and at 4.03 dollars to the pound it seemed clear that sterling had been overvalued. In 1949 Great Britain, therefore, had to devalue sterling to 2.80 US dollars to the pound. Many other countries also devalued their currencies. though not all to the same extent.

(e) *The return to convertibility*. To maximise multilateral trade, currencies must be freely convertible. It became the aim, therefore, of the British Government to restore convertibility to the pound by easy stages. The chief obstacle, however, was the inadequacy of the

British gold reserves. The severity of the British system of exchange control was gradually relaxed until, in January 1959, sterling was given free convertibility except to people resident in Great Britain.

(f) *The Group of Ten.* A feature of recent years has been the co-operation of the central banks of ten countries—the United States, Great Britain, France, West Germany, Italy, Belgium, the Netherlands, Sweden, Canada and Japan—to increase the lending resources of the IMF. In order to increase international liquidity the IMF in 1970 began to issue SDRs (Special Drawing Rights) to members in proportion to their quotas. These form part of each country's reserves.

(g) *The devaluation of sterling (1967).* Sterling crises of increasing severity occurred in 1951, 1955, 1961, 1964 and 1967, but in spite of assistance from the Group of Ten, the central banks of the United States and some other countries Great Britain was compelled in 1967 to devalue sterling to 2.40 US dollars to the pound. On this occasion only a few others did likewise.

(h) *The return to flexible exchange rates since 1972.* Until the 1960s the US dollar was widely accepted as an international means of payment, but the huge increase in the supply of US dollars finally undermined it, and in 1971 it ceased to be convertible for gold. The IMF has always strongly favoured fixed exchange rates in any revised scheme, and as a result of the Smithsonian Agreement a new set of parities, amounting in effect to a devaluation of the US dollar, was agreed in December 1971. Then in 1972 with increasing pressure on sterling its rate on the foreign exchange market was allowed to fluctuate. One by one other currencies followed. This, in effect, marked the breakdown of the system established at Bretton Woods, though the IMF continued to function. With a floating exchange rate a country's reserves are protected, but concern for the reserves is replaced by concern for the depreciation of a currency on the foreign exchange market if this becomes persistent. This was the problem with sterling during the following years, especially 1973 when its value in terms of other currencies fell by over 48%. By 1977 the pound sterling was only worth 1.70 US dollars. Throughout the period after 1945 sterling was handicapped by its role as an international means of payment even though by then it was less used for this purpose than the US dollar. Many countries holding sterling balances reduced them whenever sterling was under pressure and thereby increased Great Britain's difficulties with its balance of payments. In January 1977, however, a scheme was formulated with the co-operation of the Bank of International Settlements to protect sterling from such action and to run down the sterling balances.

QUESTIONS

1. Consider the importance of gold to the Bretton Woods scheme.

2. Why was the pound devalued in 1949?

3. Consider the advantages and disadvantages of fixed as against flexible rates of exchange.

4. Account for the return to flexible rates of exchange in 1972.

XXXII. Industrial Relations

1. Before 1825

Trade unions are combinations of workers formed for the purpose of taking collective, instead of individual, action against their employers for the betterment of working conditions. Their weapon is industrial action such as the so-called "working to rule" or the strike. As an individual the worker is weak, but by combining with his fellow-workers he can help to form a strong union. From small weekly subscriptions the unions can build up funds to assist members when on strike. Generally, however, the strike is regarded as a weapon of last resort, the more usual procedure being for the unions first to discuss their grievances with the appropriate employers' association, wage disputes being settled by collective bargaining, followed if necessary by conciliation or arbitration.

The break-up of the medieval gilds left labour unorganised. The harsh conditions of the early years of the Industrial Revolution—long hours, low wages, bad working conditions—led workers to combine together, but the Combination Acts of 1799–1801 made illegal any association formed for the purpose of raising wages or securing shorter hours. Largely owing to Francis Place, the Combination Laws were repealed.

2. 1825–70

After 1825 many unions were formed, though they were mostly small, and many strikes followed. One of the few employers of the time who supported trade unions was Robert Owen, a man inspired by great ideals.

On joining some of those early unions, members had to take an oath of secrecy and obedience. This was illegal. At Tolpuddle, Dorset, in March 1834 six farm labourers were arraigned on a charge of administering an oath to new members. Tried and found guilty, they were sentenced to seven years' transportation.

Strikes were frequent during the early part of this period, and because it was generally believed that trade unions were revolutionary in aim their progress and development were hindered. After 1845, however, the unions became less violent in character, the strike was denounced, liberal principles were accepted and the leaders began to look to Parliament for the remedying of their grievances. As a result, membership of the unions rapidly increased. The federation of local unions continued and they became more national.

3. 1871–89

Even in the late nineteenth century the law still hindered the growth of trade unions. Since they were not legally recognised, they could not secure redress in court in case of misappropriation of funds by fraudulent officials. The Trade Union Acts of 1871 and 1876 clarified the position of the unions and legalised them. These Acts gave the unions protection for their property and funds and also freed members from a possible charge of conspiracy.

"New Unionism". The years 1889–1900 were a period of great development for trade unions. Previously they had been mainly unions of skilled workers, whereas the new unions also included unskilled workers. The dockers' strike of 1889, organised by John Burns, was one of the first strikes to obtain the sympathy of the general public. The result was a big increase in the membership of the unions.

4. 1900–39

Two important legal decisions affecting trade unions were given in 1900 and 1913:

(a) *The Taff Vale Case*. In 1900 the claim of the Taff Vale Railway for damages for breach of contract by employees on strike was sustained in the courts. To give the trade unions protection and to allow "peaceful" picketing, the Trade Disputes Act was passed in 1906.

(b) *The Osborne Judgment*. A member of a union objected to part of his subscription being used for political purposes. The Trade Union Act of 1913 declared that compulsory payment for political purposes should not be allowed. In 1919 the International Labour Office (ILO) was established at Geneva to discuss labour problems at international level.

In 1926 a prolonged strike of coal-miners developed into a general strike. This failed, and in 1927 the Trade Disputes Act was passed to make such strikes illegal, but it was repealed in 1946.

A feature of the past twenty-five years has been the increasing militancy of the unions and the extension of trade unionism to "white collar" workers.

5. Types of union
There are two main types of trade union:

(a) Craft unions, whose members are skilled workers engaged in the same or closely associated occupations.

(b) Industrial unions, which accept as members all grades of workers, skilled and unskilled, in a particular industry.

In addition to providing a means of collective bargaining with their employers, most unions acted as friendly societies, offering insurance against sickness and accident before the introduction of national insurance.

6. "The closed shop"
Some trade unions insist that a firm's employees should all be members of the appropriate trade unions. Strikes have sometimes occurred when workers have refused to join the union. Many disputes of this kind have occurred in recent years. Cases have occurred of men being dismissed for refusing to join a union. In favour of the "closed shop" it is argued that those who are not members of the union should not enjoy the benefits obtained

by the union for its members. Non-unionists assert that insistence on the closed shop is an infringement of the liberty of the individual. The Act of 1975 (*see* **9** below), however, legalised the closed shop.

7. Employers' associations

These are as old as the trade unions. Employers in almost every industry now have their association, which provides them with an organisation capable of negotiating with the trade unions. The Confederation of British Industry in its relationship to the various employers' associations bears some resemblance to the relationship of the Trades Union Congress to the individual trade unions. The existence of these two bodies makes it possible for the Government to negotiate with industry as a whole.

The trade unions have proved a potent force for the protection of the interests of the employees, and the employers' associations have provided a similar service for the employers. The danger underlying the existence of two such powerful sets of bodies is that their joint interest is contrary to that of consumers.

The Bullock Report (1977) recommended that there should be worker participation in management (industrial democracy) with union representatives on the Boards of companies.

8. The trade unions and full employment

Lord Beveridge emphasised that the success of a full employment policy depended upon the displaying of an enlightened attitude towards wages by the trade unions, since full employment put them in a strong bargaining position. If trade unions take advantage of these conditions continually to press for wage increases, the result will be continuous inflation. In recent years the Government on a number of occasions has persuaded unions for limited periods to accept wage restraint, but without much success in the long run.

9. Attempts to reform the trade unions

During the 1960s the power of the trade unions greatly increased. There was too a shift of power from the national executives of the unions to the shop stewards in the factories.

The Donovan Report (1965) recommended that only registered trade unions should be allowed to strike. Parliament made two attempts to implement this section of the report. The first bill had to be withdrawn. In 1971 the industrial Relations Act was passed establishing a code of industrial practice and attempting to make the calling of strikes more difficult. There was open defiance of the Act culminating in a miners' strike and the downfall of the Government.

In 1975 the Trade Unions and Labour Relations Act actually increased the power of the trade unions.

QUESTIONS

1. Give a short account of trade unionism, and explain what you understand by the "closed shop". (A.C.A. Final.)

2. What are the economic functions of trade unions? (C.C.S. Inter.)

3. Describe the chief functions of trade unions. How do they differ from employers' associations?

XXXIII. Economic Activity of the State

1. Laissez-faire and its decline

Largely as a result of Adam Smith's influence, the early nineteenth century was a period when economists and the governing classes in Great Britain firmly believed in a policy of *laissez-faire*, i.e. non-interference by the State in the economic sphere. In both Great Britain and the United States there was a strong dislike of State control, though opinion in the United States rarely wavered from a belief in a high tariff. Circumstances eventually proved too strong for both countries. Interference by the State in the economic life of the nation has gradually increased, especially since 1945.

2. Types of State activity

At the present day, therefore, State activity covers a wide field:

(*a*) *Regulation of trade.* From the fifteenth to the eighteenth century most countries sought to regulate trade by the imposition of tariffs to restrict imports or bounties to encourage exports. Even during the heyday of *laissez-faire* all countries continued to regulate trade to some extent. Although Great Britain in the late nineteenth century came near to free trade, it eventually followed other countries, and in 1932 returned to a system of protection.

(*b*) *Protection of the worker.* The growth of humanitarianism led to the passing of Factory Acts, which restricted the employment of women and children and also reduced the length of the working day for men. Later Acts have made it compulsory to fence dangerous machinery and provide adequate ventilation, etc. It became clear later that these measures improved the efficiency of labour.

(c) *Education.* It soon became apparent that if a satisfactory system of education was required it would have to be provided by the State. At first education was regarded as a service for the individual, but nowadays it is considered in many countries primarily as a means of increasing the efficiency of labour and providing industry with a supply of trained labour.

(d) *Welfare services.* During the twentieth century other social services, in addition to education, have been greatly extended—housing, national insurance against sickness and unemployment, the provision of retirement pensions, widows' pensions and family allowances, social security benefit, and a comprehensive health service.

(e) *Control of industry.* The State has intervened where the misuse of monopoly power was feared, for example, in Great Britain, controlling railway rates, the building up of a code of common law to control limited companies, the establishment of the Monopolies and Mergers Commission and the abolition of Resale Price Maintenance, while in the United States anti-trust legislation has curbed the power of the great combines.

(f) *Public ownership of industry.* This is the most recent development of economic activity by the State. For a long time the Post Office was the only publicly owned commercial activity in Great Britain. Some seventy years ago the larger local authorities began to operate local transport services and to provide water, gas and electricity services. In 1926 the British Broadcasting Corporation was set up to take over the company that had previously been responsible for broadcasting. State ownership of industry in Great Britain, however, really dates from 1946. In many countries railways were State owned long before that. In this country the railways, waterways, some airlines, part of the road haulage and road passenger services, coal-mining, iron and steel industry and the production of gas and electricity have all been nationalised. Mainly to assist firms in financial difficulties, such as Rolls-Royce and British Leyland, the Government acquired shares in public limited companies—95% in the case of British Leyland.

(g) *Full employment.* In many countries nowadays the State is responsible for the maintenance of full employment. The British Government accepted this responsibility in 1944.

(h) *Control of the financial system.* The Bank of England was nationalised in 1946. Since that date responsibility for monetary policy has rested with the monetary authorities—the Treasury, the Chancellor of the Exchequer and the Bank of England.

3. Nationalisation

The nationalisation of the basic industries of the country was for a long time an important item in the policy of the British Labour Party. Consequently, when this party came to power in 1945 it immediately carried out its programme of nationalisation. There was further nationalisation during the 1960s and 1970s.

Arguments in favour of the public ownership of industry are:

(a) to protect consumers against abuses of monopoly power;

(b) to avoid competition where it would be wasteful, as in the supply of water, gas and electricity;

(c) where it was thought to be in the national interest, as with the Bank of England;

(d) in cases where in its early years an industry might require to be subsidised, as with the airlines;

(e) where complete reorganisation of an industry was required, as with coal-mining;

(f) where the safety of the community required it, as with the production of atomic energy.

The previous owners of nationalised industries, except local authorities, received compensation, generally in the form of Government guaranteed stocks, e.g. transport stock, gas stock, etc. These new stocks have, therefore, increased the country's "reproductive" debt.

The price policy of nationalised industries. It was generally laid down in the various nationalisation Acts that industries taken over by the State were expected to pay their way. These Acts usually state that nationalised industries should be run "in the public interest"—a vague phrase which cannot be precisely defined. Some people take this to mean, at any rate in the case of the railways, that they should be operated as a service, even though this may mean incurring heavy losses. Once, however, the principle of running at a loss has been accepted, no satisfactory test of efficiency remains. However, in 1968 it was decided that the basic railway system should be operated on commercial principles, but certain lines, not commercially viable but regarded as "socially necessary", should be subsidised. Since their nationalisation the railways have not found it possible to pay their own way.

The National Enterprise Board. This Government body was set up under the Industry Act 1975, and overlooks the State's interest in private firms receiving State assistance, such as Rolls-Royce, Ferranti and British Leyland.

4. State planning v. private enterprise

One of the main economic controversies of the present day revolves round the question whether an economy should be planned by the State or left to private enterprise. During both world wars there was extensive State control of production and distribution in Great Britain, but in both cases there was a general desire to get rid of these State controls afterwards.

No one now believes, however, in a completely unfettered *laissez-faire* policy, but supporters of a free economy believe that production should wherever possible remain in private hands and that the economic system should be governed by the price system within a social framework guaranteeing a minimum standard of living for all.

All parties agree that some planning is necessary, but wide divergence of opinion exists regarding the amount of planning that should be undertaken by the State and the amount of production that should be left to private enterprise. At one extreme there is the Communist State, the fully planned economy at least so far as production is concerned; at the other extreme is private enterprise, where there exists in the economic sphere the maximum amount of freedom compatible with the welfare of the community. Between these two extremes is the mixed system or "middle way" taken by Great Britain and other non-Communist states. Even in these countries, there is a tendency towards an extension of State planning.

5. Regional economic planning

In 1965 the British Government for the first time produced a national plan but it had to be abandoned. A certain amount of planning, however, is carried out on a regional basis, the country having been divided into ten economic planning regions. These with their capitals are: (*i*) Scotland (Edinburgh); (*ii*) Northern England (Newcastle upon Tyne); (*iii*) Yorkshire and Humberside (Leeds); (*iv*) North-west England (Manchester); (*v*) East Midlands (Nottingham); (*vi*) West Midlands (Birmingham); (*vii*) Wales (Cardiff); (*viii*) South-west England (Bristol); (*ix*) East Anglia (Norwich); (*x*) South-east England (London). Each region has a regional planning board. The aim is to allow each region to tackle problems peculiar to its area and so bring about the balanced economic development of the country as a whole.

QUESTIONS

1. Give some account of the part played by the State today in (*a*) production, (*b*) exchange. (R.S.A. Adv.)

2. Distinguish between State planning and private enterprise.

3. "The economic activities of the State have in-

creased and are increasing." How far *economically* is such increase (*a*) desirable, or (*b*) undesirable? (C.I.S. Inter.)

4. What do you understand by a mixed system?

5. Assess the importance of the State's share of production in Great Britain.

XXXIV. Social Security

1. Early development of social insurance

Germany was the first country to adopt a scheme of national insurance, Bismarck laying the foundations of the system. He introduced insurance against accidents and sickness in 1884, and widows' pensions in 1911. Salaried workers were brought into the scheme in 1913. Unemployment insurance was organised only in a few of the German states. Judged by modern standards, the benefits were extremely meagre, but the German system of social insurance became the model for the later schemes of other countries.

Many other countries adopted more or less ambitious schemes of social insurance. Though many British trade unions offered their members both sickness and unemployment benefits before the close of the nineteenth century, the development of social insurance in Great Britain really dates from the time of Lloyd George's tenure of office as Chancellor of the Exchequer, though Workmen's Compensation Acts had been passed in 1880, 1897 and 1906.

The Old Age Pensions Act 1908, gave non-contributory pensions of £0.25 per week to people of limited means on reaching the age of seventy. In 1920 these pensions were increased to £0.50 per week to allow for the fall in the value of money.

The National Insurance Act 1911, provided insurance against sickness and later against unemployment, the scheme being compulsory for all lower-paid workers. A fund, from which benefits were to be paid, was established, to which there were to be three groups of contributors—employers, employees and the State. The British worker paid less and received greater benefits than did the German worker.

In 1929 Winston Churchill added *widows' pensions* of £0.50 per week to the scheme.

The vast majority of salaried workers were outside all these schemes, but in 1937 those with annual incomes below £400 were allowed to become voluntary contributors for widows', orphans' and old-age pensions.

2. The present British scheme of Social Security

During 1939–45 plans were outlined for a more comprehensive system of social insurance embracing the entire population. The first plan was put forward by Lord Beveridge in his *Report on Social Insurance*, and in a somewhat modified form this was introduced by the Act of 1946, which also established a Ministry of Pensions and National Insurance with offices throughout the country to administer the scheme.

The chief features of the scheme are:

(a) All persons, irrespective of income and whether employed or self-employed, were brought within the scope of social insurance. As in the earlier schemes, there were to be three groups of contributors, namely, employers, employees and the State. The employees' contributions are exempt from income tax. It was a compulsory scheme, exemption being permitted only to married women, pensioners and people earning under £2 per week. To meet the increased benefits increased contributions were required.

Lord Beveridge's plan was largely based on the insurance principle that contributions should be large enough to provide the necessary funds to cover all payments to beneficiaries. The scheme as operated has, in fact, been more correctly a scheme of social security than of social insurance, since the contributions of employers and employees have always fallen short of what has been required to provide the various benefits. This has been especially the case with benefits such as retirement benefits, sick pay and unemployment pay, which have all been increased from time to time to keep pace with the rise in the cost of living. The cost of the Health Service falls almost entirely on the State.

(b) Benefits became payable for sickness, unemployment and to widows.

(c) Retirement pensions became payable to men at sixty-five and women at sixty years of age irrespective of income but subject to the beneficiary's appropriate rate of income tax.

(d) Maternity grants were introduced.

(e) Funeral grants became payable.

(f) Another innovation was the introduction of family allowances. This came into operation as a result of a separate Act which took effect from 1946. The comprehensive scheme began to operate from July 1948.

Where it is considered necessary, retirement pensions are supplemented. Since 1948 many benefits have been improved and others added. Recent developments have been the introduction of (i) an additional graduated scheme with pensions up to half average earnings during the period immediately prior to retirement; and (ii) the family income supplement available to families below a specified level of income.

3. Some economic effects

Consider some of the economic effects of the introduction of a national insurance scheme:

(a) A higher standard of health should result in greater physical fitness and greater efficiency of the workers.

(b) In a trade depression the higher rates of unemployment pay should lessen the reduction of purchasing power, and mitigate to some extent the effects by maintaining a greater demand for consumers' goods than was the case in previous trade depressions.

(c) The granting of family allowances may possibly check any tendency for population to decline in the future.

(d) The employers' contribution is in effect a tax on

the employment of labour, and unless this is accompanied by increased efficiency of the workers, it could result in a reduction in the demand for labour. In times of full employment the incidence of this payment is more likely to be on employers, but in a depression it is more likely to fall on employees.

(e) Owing to the heavy cost, especially of the Health Service, a permanent high level of taxation is required. With an ageing population the increasing cost of retirement pensions becomes an increasingly serious problem.

QUESTIONS

1. Give a brief account of the development of social security in Great Britain before 1945.

2. State the chief considerations for and against family allowances. On the assumption that they are desirable, give your reasons for thinking that they should be paid (a) by the State, (b) by employers. (C.I.S. Final.)

3. What contribution do the social services make to the standard of living in Great Britain? (G.C.E. Adv.)

XXXV. Taxation

1. Purposes of taxation

Revenue from taxation is required to cover a wide field of Government expenditure.

(a) In early days taxes were imposed to cover the cost of administration, defence and the maintenance of law and order, these being services which individuals could not adequately perform for themselves. The heaviest borrowing in peacetime occurred during 1970–78.

(b) Heavy borrowing to cover the cost of wars during the past 250 years has enormously increased the National Debt, the interest on which has become an important item of Government expenditure.

(c) The range of services provided by the State has increased very greatly in recent times. The Health Service and education are both very costly, but large sums are also required for housing, pensions, supplementary allowances, the provision of family income supplements, family allowances, a portion of this expenditure being in the form of grants to local authorities to supplement expenditure financed by local rates.

2. The budget as an instrument of economic policy

In April each year the Chancellor of the Exchequer presents his budget to Parliament. This is an estimate of State income and expenditure for the ensuing year. To balance, the budget expenditure is first estimated and then the taxes necessary to cover it are imposed. Occasionally, in time of crisis, interim budgets have been introduced. These became of more common occurrence during 1972–76.

The budget has now become an important instrument

of economic and social policy, taxes being imposed not only to cover Government expenditure. Shortly before budget day details of the country's economic position are published in a series of White Papers—the Economic Survey, National Income and Expenditure and the Balance of Payments. These indicate the type of budget the economic conditions of the time require.

Some of the ways in which the budget has been used in recent years as an instrument of economic policy are as follows:

(a) *To check inflation.* In order to reduce consumers' demand, taxation may be maintained at a higher level than is necessary to cover Government expenditure so that a large budget surplus is produced. This, however, requires indirect taxes on commodities to be generally increased, and since this raises many prices—and therefore the cost of living—the effect may be to stimulate inflation further instead of checking it.

(b) *To stimulate recovery from a trade recession.* In this case, taxes will be reduced, and a budget deficit deliberately incurred, in order to increase the volume of purchasing power and so stimulate demand.

(c) *To assist the balance of payments.* Taxes can be imposed to check particular imports or to reduce the demand generally, including the demand for imports.

(d) *To reduce inequality of incomes.* This is achieved by a progressive system of taxation, high incomes being deliberately heavily taxed, for the purpose of reducing them rather than for additional revenue.

On a number of occasions in recent years the budget has been framed in one of these ways to meet the different economic conditions of the time. Serious difficulty arises, as in the 1970s, when inflation and unemployment occur simultaneously, so that contradictory policies of deflation and monetary expansion are required at the same time!

3. Principles of taxation

Adam Smith stated four "canons" or principles of taxation: (a) equality, by which he meant that taxation should be proportional to people's incomes; (b) certainty with regard to the amount to be paid; (c) convenience of payment; (d) the cost of collection should form only a small proportion of the amount to be raised.

A country's system of taxation can be based on any one of the following general principles:

(a) *Equality of payment.* In this case there would be a fixed tax at so much per head of the population, that is, a poll tax. Taxes on the cheaper necessary foodstuffs tend to be similar to poll taxes, since they fall more or less equally on everyone.

(b) *Proportional payment.* In this case people pay taxes proportional to their incomes. For example, a person with an income of £1,500 per year might pay £150 in taxes and a person with £5,000 a year would then pay £500. Equality of payment tends to increase inequality of income and proportional payment does little to reduce it.

(c) *The principle of minimum sacrifice.* This would mean that only the wealthy would pay taxes, but this would not bring in sufficient revenue for a modern Government's needs. All Governments, whatever their political complexion, have found it necessary to tax all sections of the community.

(d) *The progressive principle.* This principle is based on the theory that the marginal utility of an economic good (including money) decreases after a certain point the more one has of it. The present British income tax is of this type. Payments are steeply graded so that people with small incomes pay a smaller proportion of their incomes in tax than the well-to-do.

Where there is great inequality of income, it is generally considered that the most equitable tax system is a progressive one, based on income. Taxes on necessary foodstuffs tend to be regressive, since people on low incomes spend a much bigger proportion of their incomes on food than the people with high incomes.

The progressiveness of British income tax can be seen

in Table XII showing the amount to be paid (in 1977–78) over a range of incomes by a married couple.

TABLE XII. *British Income Tax.*

Annual income	Income tax	Tax as % of income
£	£	£
1,500	15	1.0
2,000	185	9.3
2,500	355	14.2
5,000	1,205	24.1
10,000	3,162	31.6
20,000	9,748	48.9
25,000	13,762	54.0

4. Direct and indirect taxation

Taxes can be classified as direct or indirect. Direct taxes are taxes on income, e.g. income tax, corporation tax. Indirect taxes are those imposed on goods or services, that is, they are taxes on outlay, e.g. value-added tax and customs and excise duties.

(*a*) *Direct taxes.* Such taxes are regarded as more equitable than indirect taxes, since they can be more closely related to each taxpayer's ability to pay. Since its introduction, British income tax has become increasingly more progressive. This has been brought about by granting taxpayers certain allowances free of tax—a personal allowance, with a larger allowance for a married man than for a single person, with higher personal allowances for people of retirement age, an allowance for a wife's earned income or for a dependent relative, etc., and by assessing the higher portions of income and income from investment (above a certain amount) at a higher rate of tax.

In 1973, surtax as a separate tax was abolished and replaced by a single income tax, graduated as surtax had been to make it progressively heavier on higher incomes. A serious drawback to heavy direct taxation, however equitable it may appear to be, is its disincentive effect.

By reducing willingness both to work and to save, it has an adverse effect on economic growth.

Corporation tax is a tax on company profits. Such taxes are often criticised by economists on grounds that they are taxes on enterprise and so tend to check entrepreneurs from undertaking production where uncertainty is very great, thereby hindering economic progress. The capital transfer tax, introduced in Great Britain in 1973, imposes a graduated tax on gifts made during a person's lifetime (with certain minor exemptions) as well as on his estate at his death. Estates of less than £25,000 are free of duty, the rate then gradually rising to 75% on estates of over £2 million.

A capital gains tax is a tax on a gain made by selling some form of property (as, for example, stocks or shares), at a higher price than was paid for it. Capital gains were first fixed in Britain in 1962.

(b) *Indirect taxes.* These taxes may be specific—that is, the tax is based on a definite amount of a commodity, e.g. a gallon of petrol, or *ad valorem*, that is proportionate to the value of the commodity, e.g. value-added tax. If imposed on foodstuffs, these taxes tend to be regressive. Though not so clearly related to the ability to pay as are direct taxes, nevertheless the well-to-do will pay more than those with low incomes in indirect taxation if the taxes are placed on a wide range of commodities and levied on an *ad valorem* basis, with higher rates on "luxuries". To bring the United Kingdom in line with other members of the EEC, value-added tax (VAT) replaced purchase tax and selective employment tax in 1973. VAT is regarded as preferable to purchase tax because it can be spread over a wider area of consumption, including services as well as commodities, with only a few items exempt or zero-rated.

Since 1973 taxes imposed on imports for the sake of revenue have been known as excise duties, while only those imposed to protect home production are now known as customs duties. Often the purchaser is unaware of the exact proportion of the price formed by the tax. These are taxes on outlay as distinct from taxes on income, and how much a person pays depends, therefore, on the extent to which he consumes commodities that are taxed. To be equitable, taxes on commodities should be placed on as wide a range of goods as possible, as is the case with VAT, (although since 1975 Great Britain has had two VAT rates) so that no particular group of consumers is unfairly hit. In Great Britain a hundred years ago, about 70% of the State's revenue came from indirect taxes.

Customs duties are taxes on imports and may be imposed to raise revenue or for purposes of protection.

5. Incidence of taxation

If the imposition of a particular tax means that a person has to pay the full amount of tax, then the incidence of that tax is clearly upon that person. In the case of income tax the incidence of the tax is upon the receiver of the income so taxed, since his income is reduced by the full amount of the tax.

In the case of taxes on commodities the incidence may be upon the buyer or the seller or divided between buyer and seller, depending on the elasticity of demand for the commodity. Since generally the demand for necessaries is more inelastic than the demand for luxuries, taxes on necessaries usually raise prices more than taxes on luxuries. If demand is perfectly elastic so that the price does not rise at all the incidence of the tax is entirely on the seller; if, however, demand is perfectly inelastic the price will rise by the full amount of the tax and the incidence will be entirely on the buyer; in all other cases the incidence will be partly on the buyer and partly on the seller. Consider Table XIII which can be shown graphically as in Fig. 14.

TABLE XIII. *Incidence of Taxation.*

| | | | | Incidence | |
Commodity	Old price £	Tax £	New price £	Buyer £	Seller £
A	15	5	15	—	5
B	15	5	18	3	2
C	15	5	20	5	—

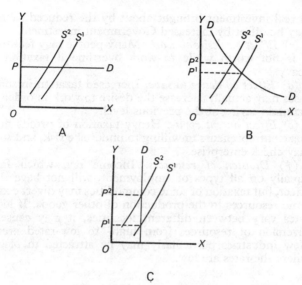

FIG. 14—*The Effect of a Tax.*

The curve S^2 shows supply after the imposition of a tax on the commodity, the effect of the tax being similar to an increase in the cost of production of the commodity. These diagrams show that, from the point of view of maximising revenue, the commodities most suitable for taxation are those for which demand is fairly inelastic, as for example, tobacco.

6. Economic effects of taxation
Taxation can affect production in a number of ways:

(*a*) *Effect on ability to work.* If necessaries of life are heavily taxed the health, and therefore the physical efficiency, of people with small incomes will be affected with a consequent falling off in total production.

(*b*) *Effect on ability to save.* Taxation will obviously reduce the amount that can be saved, but the reduction in real investment brought about by the reduced saving may be offset by increased Government investment.

(c) *Effect on desire to work.* Many people may feel that it is not worth while to work overtime if taxation is heavy.

(d) *Effect on desire to save.* Increased taxation in some cases may actually increase the desire to work in order to maintain saving at the previous level.

(e) *Effect on enterprise.* Heavy taxation of profits may make entrepreneurs unwilling to undertake risk, and so it may check enterprise.

(f) *Division of resources.* Income tax, which falls equally on all types of employment, will not have this effect, but taxation of some commodities may divert economic resources to the production of other goods. If local rates vary between different localities, it may cause a diversion of resources from high- to low-rated areas. New industries particularly may be attracted to places where the rates are low.

7. Public debts
There are two main types of public debt:

(a) *Reproduction debt.* This is debt which is covered by some real asset, as, for example, the debts incurred in order to purchase the coal-mines, gas and electricity undertakings, and the railways. If the compensation paid to the previous owners was based on a fair assessment of the real value of the undertaking the new debt created will be exactly balanced by real assets of the same value. If more industries are nationalised this type of debt will increase.

(b) *Deadweight debt.* This is debt, which is not covered by any real asset, as, for example, debts incurred in time of war. Most of Great Britain's national debt has arisen to finance wars, and so it is mostly deadweight debt.

The burden of public debts. The extent to which a public debt is a burden on the community depends on whether it is an internal or an external debt, and in the case of an internal debt, whether it is reproductive or deadweight debt. An example of an external debt is the British debt to the United States, negotiated in the Washington Agreement of 1946 and the debt incurred in 1976 to the IMF. An external debt, especially if it is large, can be a serious burden on a country, since the interest and capital repayment can be met only by exporting goods and services in exchange for which no other goods or services are received. Thus an external debt makes it more difficult to achieve a balance in the balance of payments. The British national debt is mostly an internal debt, the interest payments in this case being merely transfers from taxpayers to interest receivers, so that the total wealth of the country as a whole is not affected. The greater the debt, however, the higher the taxation required to meet it, and this may tend to increase inequality of income. On the other hand inflation, by reducing the value of money, also reduces the burden of the national debt—at the expense of holders of Government securities. As a result, the national debt was less of a burden in 1977 than it was in 1937 or even in 1967 in spite of the huge increase in the national debt since then.

The national debt. Until 1945, the history of the natio-

TABLE XIV. *Great Britain's National Debt.*

Date	£ million	Period
1694	1.2	
1714	49	End of wars of William III and Marlborough
1750	80	
1785	244	End of War of American Independence
1815	858	End of Napoleonic Wars
1853	771	Before Crimean War
1856	831	After Crimean War
1899	635	Before South African War
1902	798	After South African War
1914	656	Before First World War
1920	7,800	After First World War
1945	23,000	After Second World War
1977	49,362	

nal debt is a history of the wars in which Great Britain had been involved since 1694. The huge increase in the national debt since 1945 is unique for peace-time. Table XIV shows its growth during this period: in addition, there are the debts of local authorities which amount to over £8,000 million.

The British national debt consists of Savings Certificates, British Savings Bonds, Premium Bonds, a variety of Government stocks which are dealt in on the stock exchange, Treasury bills (the floating debt), and the external debt, owed mainly to the United States, Canada and, more recently, to the IMF.

8. Local rates

Taxes have to be paid both to the central Government and to local authorities, local taxes being known as rates. To some extent rates are a payment for services provided by the local authority, such as parks, street lighting, local roads, public libraries, etc. Local authorities, however, have to provide many services as agents for the Government—education, police, health, etc.—the cost being partly borne by the rates and partly by Government grants. In Great Britain rates are assessed on property—houses and business premises. A rateable value is assigned to all property, approximately equivalent to the value of its rent. For example, the occupier of a house with a rateable value of £32 with rates at 90p in the £ would pay £28.80 in rates.

Objections to this method of assessing rates are: (*i*) the amount to be paid varies between one area and another; the yield from a penny rate in one town may be much greater than the yield from a penny rate in another town; (*ii*) property does not form a good basis for a system of taxation: it is only indirectly related to income, and so it penalises unduly people who live in the larger houses; and (*iii*) it influences the types of houses built. Rates tend to be a regressive form of taxation, since they are not directly related to the income of each household. Since 1967, however, a rates rebate has been granted to householders in the lower income groups.

QUESTIONS

1. What do you mean by incidence of taxation? Show, by means of an illustration, how you would proceed to investigate the incidence of a tax and by what factors the incidence is affected. (I.B.)

2. Describe the basis of assessment of local rates in England and discuss the merits and demerits of the rating system. (I.B.)

3. Show the differences: (a) between rates and taxes; (b) between progressive and regressive taxes; (c) between customs duties and excise duties. (G.C.E. Ord.)

4. Outline the main sources of Government income and assess their relative importance. (G.C.E. Adv.)

5. What are the characteristics of a good tax system? Explain what is meant by (a) progressive taxation, (b) the incidence of taxation.

6. "Half the national debt consists of marketable securities; another quarter consists of National Savings; some fifteen per cent is floating debt." Why, then, is the debt spoken of as a burden? (I.B.)

XXXVI. Notes on some Leading Economists

1. Adam Smith (1723–90)

Educated at Glasgow and Oxford Universities, he later became Professor of Logic and Moral Philosophy at Glasgow. He visited Paris, where he discussed economic questions with some of the Physiocrats. He was more interested in practical problems of applied economics than economic theory. In 1776 he published his *Wealth of Nations*. This was written before the Industrial Revolution had got fully under way at a time when industry and trade were hampered at all points by a mass of Government restrictions (the mercantilist system). His book was widely read and had enormous influence.

Chief points from his work:

(a) The economic actions of individuals are inspired by self-interest.

(b) Labour is the source of all wealth, and anything having exchange value, and not merely bullion, is wealth. This led to his elaboration of his Labour Theory of Value (*see above*, XII, 1).

(c) A huge expansion of production results from the introduction of the division of labour (*see* VI, 2).

(d) He strongly advocated *laissez-faire* principles, i.e. the freeing of industry and trade from Government restrictions. This view made his work popular, as his ideas coincided with those of contemporary business men.

Criticism:

(a) Inadequate treatment of value, wages and rent. (For criticism of his Labour Theory of Value, *see* XII, 3.)

(*b*) He wrote before the development of the factory system, and before the awful conditions of work that prevailed in the early factories had discredited the *laissez-faire* policy.

2. Thomas R. Malthus (1766–1834)

He was educated at Cambridge, and then entered the Church. In 1805 he became Professor of Political Economy at Haileybury College. He was brought up in an atmosphere of revolutionary idealism, which the excesses of the French revolutionaries after 1789 discredited. In 1798 he published the first edition of his *Essay on Population*. He lived at a time when the population of the country was increasing more rapidly than ever before, though not so rapidly as it did later. He tried to show that war, famine and disease had kept down the growth of population in the past, and he feared that the population of this country, unless checked, would grow too large for the means of subsistence and so lead to a decline in the standard of living. He emphasised his point by declaring that population increased in geometrical progression, whereas output of food increased in only arithmetical progression. Before his day an increasing population had been considered by Governments as a sign of increasing national prosperity, and to many of his contemporaries Malthus appeared as an evil influence. His work was fiercely criticised and he was much abused. A second edition of his essay, published in 1803, and almost entirely rewritten, was less controversial than the first edition. In this he modified some of his earlier opinions, adding moral restraint to his other checks on the growth of population, and admitting that as the population of a country approached its limit the rate of increase gradually declined.

Criticism: he could not be expected to foresee the opening up of the vast agricultural resources of the New World, and the development of Great Britain as "the workshop of the world", and that trade between these regions would make possible a higher standard of living in Great Britain in 1900 than in 1800 in spite of a huge increase in population. Perhaps, however, the world population problem today shows that, after all, Malthus was right (*see* V, 7).

3. David Ricardo (1772–1823)

Born in London of a Jewish family, he received a commercial education. A genius for finance, he made his fortune on the stock exchange, after which he retired and took up the study of economics. In 1820 he became M.P. for an Irish constituency and had considerable influence upon opinion in the House of Commons. In 1809 he published his pamphlet *The High price of bullion: a proof of the depreciation of bank-notes*. This led to his making the acquaintance of James Mill and Malthus. In 1817 he published his *Principles of Political Economy and Taxation*. He adopted the deductive method, and the abstract character of his writing led to his often being misunderstood, but many people consider him to rank second only to Adam Smith as an economist.

Chief points from his work:

(*a*) Political economy is an inquiry into the distribution of the products of industry among the factors of production rather than an inquiry into the nature and causes of wealth.

(*b*) The value of gold depends upon its costs of production.

(*c*) He developed Smith's Theory of Value, asserting that the value of any commodity depended upon the quantity of labour required for its production.

(*d*) His chief contribution to economic theory is his theory of rent. Rent, according to him, arises as a result of differences in the fertility of land, the poorest land yielding no rent, though he recognised that advantage of situation with regard to the market was an important factor (*see* XV, 2).

Criticism: for criticism of the Ricardian Theory of Rent *see* above, XV, 3.

4. John Stuart Mill (1806–73)

He was the son of James Mill, principal official of the East India Company and author of *Elements of Political Economy*. Mill Senior made himself entirely responsible for the education of his son, who by the time he was twelve years of age had completed his study of Greek, Latin, Logic and Economics. J. S. Mill also obtained a post in the employ of the East India Company, and like his father eventually became its chief official. When in 1858 the Company surrendered its rule in India to the British Government, Mill received a pension in compensation. From an early age he had been an enthusiast for the cause of human improvement, and in 1822 founded the Utilitarian Society. In 1843 he published his *Logic* and in 1848 his *Principles of Political Economy*, which remained for a long time the standard textbook on economics. For a short period, 1865–68, he was a Member of Parliament.

Chief points from his work:

(*a*) He attempted to produce an up-to-date survey of the whole field of economics.

(*b*) He claimed to be the first to establish a distinction between (*i*) the laws of production, which cannot be modified, and (*ii*) the laws of distribution, which are liable to change with social progress.

(*c*) He developed the wages fund theory of wages (*see* above, XVI, 3), though later he abandoned it.

(*d*) He developed a theory of international trade.

Criticism: he supported the Cost of Production Theory of Value (*see* XII, 2–3), and though finality is unusual with Mill, he claimed that nothing further was to be said on the theory of value. He attached insufficient importance to the influence of demand on Value.

5. Walter Bagehot (1826–77)

Educated at University College, London, he became Vice-Chairman of Stuckey's Bank. He was both a student and a business man. For a time he was editor of *The Economist*. In 1873 he published *Lombard Street*, in which he described the working of the money market and the development of banking. This was the first serious contribution to the study of the theory of central banking.

Chief points from his work:

(a) His account of the working of the money market (*see* XXIII).

(b) The Bank of England has the only cash reserve in the country. Its pre-eminence carries the responsibility of protecting this reserve. Bagehot thought this reserve too small (*see* XXIV).

(c) Bank-rate is an instrument for protecting this reserve (*see* XXIV, 5).

(d) He tried to show that there was a connection between the expansion or contraction of bank credit and commercial crises (*see* XXVI).

6. W. S. Jevons (1835–82)

Born in Liverpool, he was educated at University College, London, where he studied chemistry. In 1854 he accepted the post of assayer to the new mint at Sydney. During 1859–62 he resumed his studies at University College, taking mathematics, economics and philosophy. In 1866 he became Professor of Political Economy at Owen's College, Manchester. His chief writings included *The Mathematical Theory of Economics* (1862), *The Coal Question* (1865), *Theory of Political Economy* (1871), and *Money and the Mechanism of Exchange* (1875). In 1878 he read before the British Association his paper propounding his celebrated "sun-spot" theory of the trade cycle. An able statistician, it was his aim "to substitute exact inquiry and exact numerical calculations for guesswork and groundless argument", with the result that he worked out a mathematical theory of economics, which he mistakenly thought he was the first to develop. He showed little respect, however, for the views of earlier writers on economics, but his work was not nearly so revolutionary as he imagined.

Chief points from his work:

(*a*) He introduced the conception of final utility i.e. marginal utility) into the theory of value (*see* XIII). He emphasised the influence of demand, whereas earlier writers had approached the problem entirely from the side of supply.

(*b*) He made a statistical study of prices, and noted the cyclical occurrence of commercial crises. He also examined the effects of the gold discoveries of 1848–50.

(*c*) Wages ultimately depend on the productivity of labour (XVI, 4).

Criticism: his bias towards a mathematical method led him to over-emphasise this aspect of the subject.

7. Alfred Marshall (1842–1924)

Educated at Cambridge, taking mathematics, he later became a lecturer there. In 1877 he accepted the post of Principal of University College, Bristol, but in 1833 he became a Fellow of Balliol College, Oxford, and lecturer in Political Economy. In 1885 he returned to Cambridge as Professor of Political Economy, retiring in 1908. A man of wide learning, he also acquired a deep knowledge of the problems of the industrial and commercial world. Unlike Jevons he had a great respect for the earlier economists, adapting the ideas of Ricardo, Mill and other early writers to the changed conditions of his own day. "Economics," he said, "is on the one side a study of wealth; and on the other and more important side, a part of the study of man." His chief work was *Principles of Economics*, the first edition of which was published in 1890. For a long time it was recognised as the standard work on economics.

Chief points from his work:

(*a*) Elasticity of demand (*see* XI, 5).
(*b*) The Principle of Substitution (*see* IX, 1).

(*c*) Quasi-rent (*see* XV, **6**).

(*d*) Internal and external economies of large-scale production (*see* IX, **3** and **9**).

8. Lord Keynes (1884–1946)

John Maynard Keynes was educated at Eton and King's College, Cambridge, reading mathematics. The greatest economist of the twentieth century, he spent some time in the Civil Service before returning to Cambridge as Fellow of King's College, where his lectures on money attracted wide attention. He represented the Treasury at Versailles (1919), was a member of the Macmillan Committee on Finance and Industry (1931) and represented the British Treasury at Bretton Woods (1945). His chief writings include *A Treatise on Money* (1930) and his most famous work, *The General Theory of Employment, Interest and Money* (1936). In the latter he challenged the classical theory of economics, since it offered no explanation or solution of the great problem of his day—mass unemployment. His theory of saving and investment became the basis of post-war policies for the maintenance of full employment.

His main contributions to economic theory were the idea of liquidity-preference, the savings–investment theory, the dependence of saving and interest on the level of income and the view that income and employment depend upon the level of investment and the propensity to consume.

For a long time his work caused great controversy. In the practical field his idea that demand should be stimulated to check unemployment found favour in Great Britain in the 1940s and in the United States in the 1960s. Recently, however, doubts have been expressed in some quarters as to the relevance of his views to the great inflations of the 1970s.

Books for further Reading

General textbooks
J. L. Hanson, *A Textbook of Economics*, Macdonald and Evans 1977.
R. G. Lipsey, *An Introduction to Positive Economics*, Weidenfeld and Nicolson 1973.

Principles of economics
K. E. Boulding, *Economic Analysis*, Harper and Row 1966.
Joan Robinson, *The Economics of Imperfect Competition*, Macmillan 1969.
Sir J. R. Hicks, *The Social Framework*, Oxford University Press 1971.
Lord Beveridge, *Full Employment in a Free Society*, Allen and Unwin 1960.

Money and banking
R. S. Sayers, *Modern Banking*, Oxford University Press 1967.
Lord Keynes, *The General Theory of Employment, Interest and Money*, Macmillan 1963.
Sir D. Robertson, *Money*, Nisbet 1968.
J. L. Hanson, *Monetary Theory and Practice*, Macdonald and Evans 1978.

International trade
B. Whale, *International Trade*, Frank Cass 1967.

Taxation
H. Dalton, *Principles of Public Finance*, Routledge and Kegan Paul 1967.
U. K. Hicks, *Public Finance*, Nisbet 1951.

A. R. Prest, *Public Finance in Theory and Practice*, Weidenfeld and Nicolson 1975.

Social economics
W. Hagenbuch, *Social Economics*, Nisbet 1958.

The history of economic thought
Sir E. Roll, *A History of Economic Thought*, Faber and Faber 1973.

INDEX

Accepting houses, 135
Accumulation of capital, 30
Advances, Bank, 127, 133
Ageing population, 24
American loan, 185
Applied economics, 4
Assets, Bank, 131–3
Automation, 30

Bagehot, W., 217
Balance of payments, 162–5
Balance sheet, Bank's, 131–3
Bank Charter Act (1844), 140
Bank deposits, 111, 126
Bankers' deposits, 144
Bank-notes, 110–11, 126, 143
Bank of England, 140–7
Bank-rate, 145–6
Banks, 124–34
Bargaining theory, 93
Barter, 109
Benefits, National Insurance, 201
Beveridge, Lord, 21, 48, 157, 191, 200
Bills of exchange, 127, 133, 136
Blocked accounts, 181
Bonus shares, 149
Branch banking, 133–4
Branded goods, 78
Bretton Woods Agreement, 183
Brokers, 152
Budget, 203–4
Building Societies, 151
Bullock Report (1977), 191
Burns, John, 189

Capital, 27–32, 44, 149–51
Capital consumption, 31
Capital gains tax, 207
Capital market, 149
Capital movements, 174
Capital transfer tax, 207
Cartel, 79

Cash Ratio, 129
Central bank, 140
Choice, 6, 7, 8
Circulating capital, 149
Clearing House, 129
Close company, 40
"Closed shop", 190
Coinage, 109–10
Collateral security, 129
Combination Acts, 188
Combines, types, 78
Commercial banks, 124–5, 135
Common Market, European, 169
Comparative costs, Principle of, 159–61, 167
Competitive demand, 60
Competitive supply, 67
Composite demand, 60
Consols, 11
Consumers' goods, 27
Convertibility, 184, 185
Convertibility Crisis (1947), 185
Co-operative societies, 41
Co-ordination of factors of production, 43
Corporation tax, 207
Cost of living, 95, 121–3
Cost of production theory of value, 70
Costs, 51–2, 74, 103
Credit, 128–30
Currency and Bank Notes Act (1928), 141
Current accounts, 126

Deadweight debt, 210
Debentures, 41, 149
Deflation, 163
Demand, 57–62
Demand, changes in, 64–6, 68–9
Demand curves, 58
Demand for money, 118
Demand schedules, 57

Deposit accounts, 126
Depreciation, 12, 163, 177
Derived demand, 60
Descriptive economics, 4
Devaluation, 163, 175, 185, 186
Devaluation of Sterling, 185, 186
Diminishing marginal utility, 72–3
Diminishing Returns, Law of, 16, 21, 51
Direct taxation, 206
Discount Houses, 135
Discriminating monopoly, 80
Distribution, 86
Distribution of Industries Act (1945), 48
Division of labour, 28
Division of labour, International, 159
Donovan Report (1965), 192
Double counting, 12
Dumping, 80, 167

Economic policy, 4
Economic theory, 4
Economic welfare, 11
Education, 19, 194
Efficiency of labour, 19
Elasticity of demand, 60–2
Employers' associations, 191
Entrepreneur, 34–8
Equilibrium price, 64
Equilibrium theory, 73
European Economic Community (E.E.C.), 169
European Free Trade Area, 169
Exchange control, 163, 179
Exchange Equalisation Accounts, 180
Export duties, 168
External economics, 47

Factors of production, 14–15
Factory Acts, 19, 193
Fiduciary issue, 111, 140
Finance Companies, 126, 151
Finance for Industry, 151
Financing of industry, 149–51
Fixed capital, 149
Fixed costs, 52
Flexible exchange rates, 177, 187
Floating exchange rates, 177, 187
Food and Agriculture Organisation, 23
Free trade, 166
Full employment, 21, 157–8

Functions of banks, 126–7
Functions of money, 112

GATT, 170
General Strike, 190
Giffen goods, 59
Gold, 115, 119, 144, 171–5
Gold bullion standard, 172
Gold exchange standard, 172
Gold flows, 174
Gold standard, 171–5
Gold standard, breakdown of, 175
Government control, 8, 193–6
Government stocks, 11
Great Depression, 20
Gresham's Law, 110
Group of Ten, 186

Health Service, 201
Hedging, 37
Highly-organised markets, 55
Hire purchase, 127, 147
Holding company, 79
Horizontal combines, 78
Hyperinflation, 119

Imperfect competition, 75
Imperfect markets, 55
Import duties, 168
Import quotas, 168
Incidence of taxation, 208
Income tax, 206
Increasing returns, 51
Index numbers, 121–2
Indirect taxation, 206, 207
Industrial Development Act (1966), 49
Industrial fluctuations, 154
Industrial Revolution, 3, 28, 31, 48
Infant industries, 166
Inferior goods, 59
Inflation, 94, 119–20
Insurance, 36, 150
Interest, 98–101
Internal economics, 44–5
International Bank, 184
International Monetary Fund, 164, 183–4, 186, 211
International trade, 159
Inventions, 96
Invisible items in balance of payments, 162–3, 165
"Iron Law" of wages, 90

Jevons, W. S., 218
Jobbers, 152
Joint demand, 59
Joint-stock banks, 124–5, 135
Joint-stock companies, 39–40
Joint supply, 67

Kartell, *see* Cartel
Kennedy Round, 170
Keynes, Lord, 100, 220

Labour, 18, 22, 44
Labour supply, 18
Labour theory of value, 70
Laissez-faire, 193
Land, 15–17, 43
Large-scale production, 44–7
Legal tender, 110
Lender of Last Resort, 144
Liabilities, Bank's, 131
Limited Company, 39–40
Liquidity, 128–30
Liquidity-preference, 99
Liverpool Cotton Exchange, 55
Loans, Bank, 127, 128
Local authority enterprise, 41, 84
Local Employment Act (1960), 49
Local rates, 212
Location of industry, 47–50
London Wool Exchange, 55
Long-term interest rates, 100

Malthus, T. R., 16, 21, 22, 23, 215
Marginal cost, 76
Marginal productivity, 43, 91, 93
Marginal revenue, 76
Marginal utility, 72
Market price, 64
Markets, 54–6
Market theory, 91–2
Marshall, A., 71, 219
Marshall Plan, 185
Marx, K., 70
Mass unemployment, 20, 24
Medium of exchange, 109, 112
Merchant banks, 126
Methods of economic study, 4
Mill, J. S., 70, 90, 217
Mobility of factors of production, 18, 43
Monetary policy, 145–7
Money, 32, 109–12

Money market, 135–9
Monopolies and Restrictive Practices Commission, 83
Monopoly, 75–84
Multiplier, 156

National Debt, 25, 211
National Income, 11–13, 86, 119
National Insurance Act (1911), 199
National Plan, 197
Nationalisation, 84, 195–6
New towns, 49
"New Unionism", 189
Nominal wages, 90
Non-specific factors of production, 15
Normal price, 64
Note issue, 111, 126, 143

Oil, 164
Old Age Pensions Act (1908), 199
Open-Market operations, 146–7
"Opportunity cost", 7
Optimum firm, 50
Optimum population, 22–3, 25
Ordinary shares, 40
Osborne Judgment, 190
Overdraft, 127
Owen, Robert, 188

Paper money, 110
Partnership, 39
Perfect competition, 75
Perfect markets, 54
Piece-rates, 94–5
Planning, State, 196
Population problem, 23–4
Population, theory of, 21–3
Preference shares, 40, 41
Prime cost, 52
Private company, 40
Producers' goods, 27
Production, Volume of, *see* National Income
Profit, 102–4
Profit sharing, 95
Progressive taxation, 205
Promissory note, 136
Protection, 166–8
Public company, 40
Public debts, 210
Public deposits, 143
Public enterprise, 41, 84

Public utilities, 84
Purchasing power parity theory, 178
Pure profit, 102–4

Quantity theory, 116–17
Quasi-rent, 88
Quotas, 168

Railway charges, 83
Rate of interest, 98–101
Rate of yield, 100
Rates, Local, 212
Real wages, 90
Regional Employment Premium, 49
Rent, 86–9, 104
Reproduction debt, 210
Residual unemployment, 21
Restriction, 181
Restrictive trade practices, 83
Retail Prices, Index of, 121–3
Ricardo, D., 15, 16, 70, 86, 87, 216
"Rights" issue, 149
Risk, 36–7
"Roundabout" production, 29
Royal Commission on Equal Pay, 98

Saving, 99
Saving–investment theory, 156
Savings banks, 125
Scales of preference, 8
Scarcity, 6, 71
Seasonal employment, 20
Selling costs, 52
Sex Discrimination Act (1975), 97
Shares, 40–1
Short-term rate of interest, 100
Smith, Adam, 3, 28, 70, 193, 204, 214
Social security, 19, 25, 199–202
Social wealth, 10
Sole proprietor, 39
Special deposits, 147
Specialisation of labour, 19
Specie points, 171
Specific factors of production, 14
Speculation, 152
State enterprise, 42, 193–6
Stock Exchange, 56, 151–2
Strikes, 20, 93
Structural unemployment, 20, 24
Subsistence theory of wages, 90
Substitution, Principle of, 43

Supplementary costs, 52
Supply, Changes in, 67, 68–9
Supply curves, 62–3
Supply of money, 117, 120
Surtax, 205

Taff Vale Case, 189
Tariffs, 163, 166, 168
Taxation, 203–12
Taxation, Principles, 204
Time-rates, 94–5
Tolpuddle labourers, 188
Trade credit, 128
Trade Cycle, 154–6
Trade Disputes Acts, 189, 190
Trade Union Acts, 189
Trade unions, 93, 94, 121, 188–92
Transfer earnings, 88
Treasury bills, 136
Treasury directive, 147
Trusts, 79

Uncertainty, 36
Unemployment, 19–21
Unit investment trusts, 31, 150
Utility, 72

Value, 70–1
Value-Added Tax (VAT), 207–8
Value of money, 114–23
Variable costs, 52
Vertical combines, 78
Volume of production, see National Income

Wage drift, 96
Wage-rates, 94–6
Wages, 88, 90–7
Wages fund theory, 90
"Waiting", 29
Washington Agreement (1946), 185, 211
Wealth, 10
Weekly Return (Bank of England), 142–3
"Weighting", 121
Welfare, 11, 194
Women's wages, 96–7

Yield, rate of, 100